Whose Side

Disloyal Bonding & Strategic Lies

Bob Morrell & Jeremy Blake

A

Publication

By the Same Authors:

- *The Death of Late Space: Your Guide to Success in Media Sales*
- *The Perfect Storm: 30 Ways to Drive Your Business*
- *The Brexit Manager (or Navigating Unchartered Waters)*
- *Open All Hours: The Reality of Omni-Channel Retailing*
- *Selling The Sun: The Reality of Omni-Travel*

www.realitytraining.com
Copyright © 2024 Bob Morrell & Jeremy Blake
Editor: Ed Handyside (Cornerstones)
All rights reserved.

Table of Contents

Preface: Why This Book? 5

Prologue: The Disloyal Bonding Day 11

Chapter 1: Where Disloyal Bonding and Strategic Lies Come From 21

Chapter 2: Disloyal Bonding on the Phone (Contact Centres & Major Brands) 31

Chapter 3: Disloyal Bonding in Face-to-Face Selling 45

Chapter 4: Disloyal Bonding in Face-to-Face Service 55

Chapter 5: Disloyal Bonding in Production, Pre-Meditated Disloyal Bonding... 63

Chapter 6: Disloyal Bonding and the Strategic Lies of Head Offices 69

Chapter 7: Disrupting the Disruptors – Your Heads of Disloyal Bonding & Strategic Lies and Your Wider Disloyal Bonding Cells 81

Chapter 8: Recruiting for Integrity 87

Chapter 9: Training for Loyalty 95

Chapter 10: The Effort of Removal, Recovery and Growth 103

Chapter 11: The Restaurant – Reboot 107

Chapter 12: Tailor Made Service 111

Chapter 13: Integrity at the Heart of Insurance 119

Chapter 14: Loyal and Valuable 123

Chapter 15: Ten Takeaways 127

Epilogue: How It Really Should Be 131

Final Word 137

Preface: Why This Book?

'I would prefer even to fail with honour,
than to win by cheating.'
– *from Philoctetes by Sophocles*

For the last twenty years we have been training salespeople. This often involves listening to calls in contact centres, watching field salespeople engage with their customers, reading transcripts from web chat conversations and observing and assessing retail interactions of all types. As a company, we have trained tens of thousands of customer-facing people across the UK, Europe, the United States and Asia. Once you've seen, read, or heard 2000+ customer interactions, assessed them and reported on them, or trained thousands of people and watched their roleplays and natural abilities, you start to notice distinct and familiar patterns of behaviour. As a sales and management trainer and coach, you realise that some habits are conscious, and some are not.

One of the most common behaviours we have observed, is resorting to Disloyal Bonding. To be clear, this term means, *bonding with the customer in a way that is clearly and explicitly working with that customer, against your own organisation*. It is a form of dishonest behaviour, but unlike a lie, this one has many layers of dishonesty, all masquerading as a favour.

The term *disloyal*, is also essential to consider. Loyalty to one's work is an abstract concept. 'They're paying me, but it's a means to an end so am I truly loyal to them? Do

I need to be? Who is them? A boss? A CEO? A faceless brand?' Surely, the majority of employees, whilst glad of the work, or at least the income, will have, at best, an ambivalent feeling towards their employer. 'Surely, I can say anything to the customers, pretty much, whatever works, to hit my target and give the customer what they want?' Except, that many employers expect their staff to love their company in a way that is unnatural, and if that were not difficult enough, they should also be ambassadors for it, and live their work lives according to an often poorly chosen set of values, that underpin the company's badly written and impossible 'mission'.

To make matters more complex, a new measure, over the last 15 years, has been introduced which feeds the need for Disloyal Bonding, because the customer's rating of what you do, is now, even more important. This is NPS, or Net Promoter Score, and there are other CSAT/Customer Satisfaction measures and third-party websites where customers are invited to review their customer experience, which as we will see, is badly affecting behaviours and skewing what we think our customers are feeling about our company.

Why talk about *Strategic Lies*? Very often, Disloyal Bonding is not just a habit or an unconscious behaviour, but a policy, a cynical, money grabbing strategy designed to increase revenues at the expense of integrity. This could come from the very top of a huge company and cascade down to managers who are expected to enact this policy and if they are not careful, sell their souls at the same time.

Why is this book about *Whose side are you on?* Because, if you don't understand what Disloyal Bonding is, how it infects an organisation or how you do it yourself without thinking, then over time, your business will develop a negative reputation. That damaging perception will be being reinforced by your own staff and will eventually damage your business and where you think it's going, when you thought they were on your side!

One business publisher we approached with this book cynically suggested that business leaders were aware of the lies their staff were telling and were perfectly happy to let this continue as long as they, the leaders, benefitted. We disagree with this perspective. Life is tough enough without being continually lied to, systematically. This book is about the importance of integrity, and how you generate that reputation as a business. If your people are killing that endeavour, you will soon be a company that has no integrity, or potentially a failing brand or business that cannot understand why it doesn't make any money.

The term 'Disloyal Bonding' was coined by Jeremy Blake. We kept on hearing these expressions like 'I've got nothing to do with the pricing...' or 'these letters are generated by computer, let me see what I can do...' or 'I used to be able to give you an offer...' or 'if you tell me you've seen the internet rate...' and he was trying to define it. You're saying something to the customer that deflects blame for the policies and pricing, the apparent lack of ethics, as though you're just being paid to do this job by circumstance, with no personal attachment whatsoever to the strategy. Disloyal Bonding perfectly describes this habit, and it's a habit that is going on right now. Either you are encouraging it, your managers are, or your people are unconsciously resorting to it and no one is noticing. It could be worse than that: those who *don't* use Disloyal Bonding, may show signs of poorer performance, for which you are penalising them, even though they are defending the integrity of your brand, when their higher performing colleagues are betraying it, and yet being rewarded for it. This opens a wider debate about what kind of performance you really want. Short term sales performance that comes at a low cost, giving low profitability with scant chance of business being renewed and retained, doesn't sound like a 'sales performance' to us. You and your managers may well be disciplining people for poor performance, simply because they refuse to mislead your customers. You thought, naively, that as a manager you were on the side of the angels. High staff turnover? Rewarding the wrong behaviours like Disloyal Bonding may be contributing to that turnover, which is one of your highest costs.

In this book, we will give you many clear examples of Disloyal Bonding in action, and you will want to take immediate action to stop your staff, managers, and yourself from using it. That will be easier said than done: this is a major habit shift for millions of people. But it starts here. With this book. Understanding it and strategising a change programme to eliminate it, whilst you still can, would be the most positive outcome for you and your business. Thanks for reading.

Prologue: The Disloyal Bonding Day

Humanity is a species that thrives on habit. Our day-to-day existence hinges on a series of things, places and experiences that define our indulgencies, our treats, our tasks, our work, our exercise, and our down-time: we reach out for utensils in our kitchen; we know where the biscuits are; we know if there's enough milk; we know when we need to shop and when we need to prioritise other things.

Let's take a typical man, who runs a business, and on some Friday mornings, he treats himself to a cooked breakfast, served to him at a local café. This is not a chain café, this is an independent, which offers premium coffee and a huge plate of fried meat and eggs for a reasonable price. This has been a habit of some years, and the man gets the satisfaction of knowing that through his custom he is helping a local business. Additionally, this is a man who has taken on board the messages about climate change and wants to do his bit to save the World. One such Friday, he sits in his café, content after a huge breakfast washed down with a mug of tea, and as he sits there, considering his dessert, he notices the queue of people waiting for takeaway coffees. The harassed young server behind the counter is moving swiftly and expertly to deliver ground coffee in its various forms to the thirsty and energy-craving locals.

Engaging his brain, the man decides to get his own coffee to take away and, once the queue has dispersed, he approaches. 'What can I get you?' asks the Barista,

'Erm, a black Americano, to go, please'.

Springing into action grabbing a cardboard cup, he is asked, 'Would you like a cake?'

There is a pause. 'Oh yes! sorry, erm… okay, twist my arm, no not really, erm… millionaires shortbread please?'

He is quickly served the slice of chocolate and caramel delight, whilst the coffee is made.

In his eagerness to eat the sweet, shortbread slice, he leans forward to grab a morsel, and notices some wording on the cardboard cups. 100% Recycled. This makes him feel even more positive about his choice of café and his decision to buy a coffee and a cake and confirms his loyalty. As the Barista serves the steaming cup he can't resist. 'I see your cups are recycled… can I ask, are your lids compostable too?'.

'Sorry?'

'Your lids'… He points 'Are they compostable?'

'Oh, the lids… why do you ask?'

"Well, look, your cups say 100% recycled – I wondered if the lids are biodegradable?'

'Oh, *recycled*!' there is a laugh. 'If only I could recycle it all. It's not down to me. Nothing is recycled here – all goes in the same sack!' They point towards an overflowing black sack hung on the door handle to the back room. There are used cups and lids in evidence.

It takes a few seconds for the man to understand the magnitude of what has been said. 'Hang on, so you have cups that are recyclable, and lids that might be compostable, but you don't recycle anything?' The server looks at him as a professor would look at an annoying student who mistakenly thinks he's a genius. 'You are correct, sir. £4.85 please'.

As the man leaves the coffee shop, the irony of what has happened is only just seeping in. So, this café, one he's been using for years, buys recycled cups, in an attempt to seem environmentally friendly, adds lids, then callously throws them all away, presumably to go to landfill. How shocking!

Ahead of him, he has a busy day. He must take his car in for a repair, buy a suit for his son, sort out some insurances then go out for dinner later - not forgetting to buy some food at some point and do some actual work. As he arrives at the car dealership that is assessing his car, he is met at the service desk by an experienced service manager in a dark suit. He is the type who looks like he has seen it all, and probably has.

As he checks the car in, the man explains the problem. 'So, you see, it's a hybrid, but it's just not charging properly, so I am assuming it's something to do with the battery?'

The Service Manager doesn't hesitate. 'Yeah, well those earlier models have got the old battery technology, haven't they, before it all changed?... Ooh, 2015?' He shakes his head and gives a sharp intake of breath. 'They were dreadful. You're lucky it's lasted this long really... Cost a fortune to put right, too. Still, you never know... we'll have a look...'

As the man leaves the dealership, he has a growing sense of dread. Not just the impending cost of an expensive repair, but also the dawning realisation that the car he has bought, which he believed was a high-quality piece of Scandinavian engineering, is actually an out-of-date model, which is presumably why the person he bought it from, sold it to him. That has just been confirmed by one of the car maker's own employees, who didn't reassure in any way, and has now put the fear of God into the customer. As he starts the loaner car (not Scandinavian - it's a VW) he gently pulls out into the traffic.

Next, shrugging off this tension, he sees his son waiting for him in the High Street. These days, the sixth form in many schools and colleges all over the country dispense with the formality of a uniform, mistrust their students to dress themselves and insist on various forms of business attire. A suit is required.

In the high street menswear shop, they are served by a tailoring old boy, who has been lazily serving people with middle of the range, off-the-peg suits or thirty years. As his son emerges from the dressing room in a smart, blue, three-piece, the man is emotional. Firstly, he has never seen his son looking so smart. Secondly, the suit is very high quality, deep blue and looks high priced. 'How much is this one?' he enquires.

Quick as a flash, the assistant comes back with '£199'. The previous suit was only £149, but was a bit loose, and this one is a step up, in every sense. What's £50 here or there for his son to look this good? Isn't it worth every penny? The old boy watches the thought process for a bit and then decides to help the man out. He sidles over and whispers, conspiratorially, 'Tell you what, if you can wait till next week, that same suit is 30% off!' The smile means that he thinks he's doing the customer a favour. 'Thanks, well...we may as well wait until then.' The man and his son leave the tailors, slightly crestfallen. This sharing offends the man's sense of integrity. He could have bought it then, but then why waste money? He could go back next week, but something shifts, the moment has gone. Maybe the suit was not worth the money even with the 30% discount? Maybe the suit has been devalued in the buyers' eyes and the opportunity just doesn't happen because the salesperson didn't seize the moment and sell them the suit. Next week, because they've run out of time, they will buy two sub-standard, less well-fitting suits, online.

Arriving back at home, the man decides to kill two birds. He will call his car insurance company, as he's had a renewal quote that is too high, and he needs to renew his travel insurance because he wants to take the family to Spain and his current family policy is also up for renewal.

The call to the car insurance company goes without a hitch. He explains that his renewal quote is too high, and he doesn't want to pay so much. The agent quickly comes up with a lower price for exactly the same policy. 'Can you do any better than £287?' There is a pause. 'Let me see what I can do...tell you what, *he says in a stage whisper,* 'if you tell me, you've seen a cheaper quote on a comparison site, then I can let you have the web rate of £250....'

The man dutifully plays the game and secures the lower premium. Before the call is finished, he is asked to complete a customer survey. So pleased is he, that he has got such a discount that he scores the advisor a 9 out of 10, when usually he only ever gives people 8's.

At the same time his travel insurance renewal is going quickly, via webchat. 'My renewal is £150 per year – I want to pay less.' He is offered a straight renewal for £130. 'No, still too much,' he argues with the faceless company.

'Can you do it for £99?' There is a long wait. 'No sorry, we can't match that rate, our prices are based on offering full and comprehensive cover to five people, worldwide for twelve months. Very sorry. We can't do it for that price. £130 is our final offer.'

He decides to say no and look elsewhere. At the end of this fruitless exchange, he is asked to rate this service level, too. Annoyed and piqued at their unwillingness to budge he scores them a 3, knowing he will be noted as a detractor and that the Chat advisor will probably be disciplined for this rating as a result.

Suddenly, the phone rings, it is a broadband company offering to take over the man's broadband line for less money than he is currently paying. The pitch is simple and instant: 'We can do your broadband for £20 per month – we're the cheapest broadband on the market.'

The man ponders. Does he want 'cheap' broadband? Cheap could mean 'rubbish'? He decides to play along. 'What speeds could you offer me?' This involves a line test that is fraught with delay.

'Sorry,' says the salesperson. 'My system is really slow today...', not realising that this does not bode well for a broadband sales call. The offer is a guaranteed 80mb per second. Wow, that's quite fast.

'When could you switch me over?' he asks.

'Ooh, well, it could be four to six weeks at this rate, and then there's any notice you need to give your current provider, so it's going to be a couple of months once we've managed to get you an engineer...'. The advisor means, that they're so busy installing broadband because of high demand, it's tough to book an engineer.

Sadly, the tone used sounds like the company's own system and the slowness of the company's own service is to blame for the lack of engineers. The man passes on this opportunity. Not on price of course, but because there's too many alarm signals going off – triggered by the company's own salesperson, unwittingly thinking that explaining about his system being very slow and about a delay in delivery, is better than defining the actual easy switchover process which could have got him the sale.

As the man drives home that evening, he pops into the supermarket to buy some pizzas for the teenagers, as he and his wife are going out for dinner. The supermarket now has eight new robot cashiers, all manned by one person, a lady in her sixties, who is not impressed by the new technology. As the man scans the pizzas, a cheeky chocolate bar and an emergency bottle of red, there is a warning that comes up. The lady walks over.

'Sorry, sorry, yes I need to fiddle with the damn thing... ooh these things are bloody useless! Useless they are. I'm spending all my time keying in barcodes, confirming people's age – are you over 18? Of course you are! My feet are killing me...'

She then goes off to help someone else who is being told 'place your item in the bagging area' by a disembodied voice, and is shouting at the machine...

That evening, the man and his wife sit down in a lovely pub for dinner. The waitress walks over.

'Hiya, just to say we're very busy tonight, the Chef's up against it, so there's a minimum half hour wait for food...' She raises her eyes to the heavens as if to say 'typical'. The man orders some drinks. He then asks a question, 'Where do you get your steaks from?'

This stumps the waitress. 'No idea. Why?'

'I just wondered if you sourced them from a local farm or something like that?'

She goes off to check, whilst finding out the soup of the day and to bring the drinks. It turns out that the meat is supplied by a central company who supplies the whole chain.

The meal is slow in terms of service. Eventually they order desserts. 'I noticed the apple pie on my way in – and I see you have sticky toffee pudding on the menu, are they home-made?'

There is a pause. 'No.'

'Okay then, what are they like?'

'I don't eat desserts. I've no idea.'

That same evening, whilst they are out at dinner, an emergency meeting is being held in the insurance company where the man renewed his car insurance.

'Our conversion rate is dropping,' says the Commercial Director. 'For every hundred calls we get, we're only saving thirty-three customers. That's poor. We need to get it up to 50% at least, or we're losing money… plus we're selling too many policies at rock bottom rates, so our revenue is being hit. Big time.'

Listening to this, the Sales Manager has a solution. 'That's okay, I'll have a chat with the teams, let me see what I can do…'

'Well, what can you do?'

'We need to make the customer feel like we're doing them a special favour, something only they are being offered, and no-one else – leave it with me. We'll add something - an incentive, a smaller discount, or give them some kind of kids' toy?'

The next day a missive will be sent to team leaders instructing the new offers available for agents to use to persuade customers to stay. There are vague threats made about increasing conversion rate, NPS (customer satisfaction) is effectively abandoned except for those who stay (customers who get what they want).

The next day, a call centre advisor is given a stern verbal warning for defending his company's right to raise prices and talking about the brand and what it stands for, rather than quickly discounting, only to go on and lose that customer. He can't understand why he is being disciplined. He is hugely demotivated and sees his fellow teammates as a bunch of liars and con-artists unworthy of the title 'salesperson' because they are feeding and perpetuating the strategic lies of the company.

This man will soon leave behind the poor integrity of his corporate employer and start his own, successful business, and his former brand will never know what talent and strength they let slip through their fingers. He could have created a new successful division for them. He could have trained every person to sell with integrity. But now he does it all for himself and views his previous employer with incredulous suspicion whenever they are mentioned. If anything, they showed him what not to do.

Back to the man's Disloyal Bonding Day. That night, his mind is awash with the conversations of the day he's experienced. As he slips into a troubled sleep, he reflects that almost everything he has been through, has been really rubbish. Plus, it's been like that for a long time, and it's getting worse.

As he drifts off to sleep, the last thing he thinks is 'at least the travel insurance people had some bloody integrity.'

Chapter 1: Where Disloyal Bonding and Strategic Lies Come From

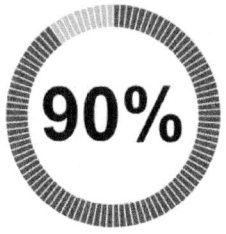

90% of salespeople don't practice honesty

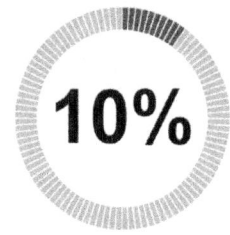

The top 10% practice honesty as the best long-term sales strategy

The top 10 percent of salespeople practice honesty as the best long-term strategy to build business and profits.
'Honesty Sells: How to Make More Money and Increase Business Profits', Steven Gaffney

If disloyal bonding exists in your organisation, then you need to get under the culture to find out why it is there.
Jeremy Blake, Reality Training, from his original article, December 2019

There are 9 million+ salespeople in the US

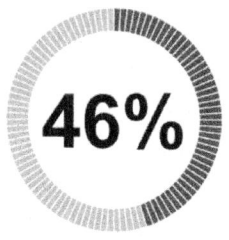

46% never intended to be salespeople

46% of salespeople didn't intend to go into sales. That makes 4.14 million accidental sales pros in the U.S.
Hubspot

If my job is to serve customers, then I am going to want them to like me. This is the fundamental condition at the heart of this subject. We all want to be liked, and we don't want customers to tar us with a brush that they may be using to paint our entire company. So, rather than defend our company, their strategy and principles, it is far easier to side with the customer. This takes the form of a lie. Rather than do my job, I will create a brief but sure image of a corrupt and poorly run company, and through this you (the customer) will have some sympathy with me, and feel like I'm doing you a favour, a one off, which ties us together briefly as friends. I will sound like I am doing you a favour, even though I am definitely not, (because there is a clear condition attached), and you will, in turn, do *me* a favour, and buy my product or service (that's the condition). It is a kind of under-the-counter reciprocity, a façade that makes both sides feel slightly odd, but not that bothered to stop themselves from behaving like this.

Also, once this works, and I hear the customer agree to this brief and definite bond between us, I think it will work again. And again. Customer after customer buying, not just because they want the product or service, but because they are playing along with the fiction that they and I are the same, that we're briefly friends, that it's not my fault, and we are both conspiring against, and sticking it to, 'the man', 'the owners', 'the corporate beast'. Through buying this thing, with my help, the customer is getting something that 'the man' would not be that happy about, but I don't care that much, as long as I've pleased you, my friend of a few minutes. The customer must know that what I have said is running my company down, criticising those in charge, but they're prepared to look past that if it means they get a good price. Never mind if it leaves a bad taste in the mouth. Never mind if, over time, this company develops a reputation as a discount shop and every conversation they have knocks a bit of money off to the point where profitability is in question and no-one can understand why this company has such a bad reputation for service and integrity.

There are three main reasons for this behaviour, psychologically.

1. If I work in retail or a contact centre as an assistant or advisor or if I am a junior salesperson in a business-to-business role, then my wages will be low. I will need to be trained and then my employer will hope that I will flourish when it comes to serving customers. If I am on a minimum wage with minimal benefits then much as I appreciate the job, I will feel very little loyalty to my employer, to the extent that, when faced with a complainer or a price related objection or any challenges that relate to *value*, it feels quite right to abdicate any responsibility and pretend to do them a special favour, agree to their demands without question or to blame a faceless system for the reason I can't give them what they want. Either way, I'm saying 'it's not me'. It's like I want them to feel sorry for me and buy something out of pity. It's a little bit pathetic.

Also, if the company is selling things or services for £500+ that's probably more than I am earning every week. To see order after order placed on the system when I am in receipt of a paltry sum, also makes me feel less likely to talk about the value because I can't see it myself. In the very worst cases, I may be so unhappy that I actively run down the company on every possible occasion. 'You're complaining? I used to earn way more, but they've changed the incentives, changed the discounts so we can't earn as much. So as far as I'm concerned, I'm going to let you have this for the price you want, and I'll let them sort it out at their end.' There it is, we're bonding against the company. I think the customer will prefer this way of behaving. Some will of course, because I'm giving them what they want, but they must also question my motives? I am allowing myself to compromise my position, and that of the company too. The customer can't see me (unless it's a virtual contact centre – they're coming!) and they don't know me. We're not going to meet for a drink or celebrate a special moment together or share a holiday. Our relationship will last the length of this one transaction.

2. The next reason is the certain fact that I have seen and heard my colleagues using similar tactics, and their results look pretty good, so I'm going to copy them. If the company management has never pulled them up before for using these techniques then they won't mind me using them either. This is learnt behaviour, because in time I will come to know that a certain percentage of customers will buy because they need

to, and also if the price is low enough; so this type of disloyal behaviour is pointless for the already price-focused customer, I'm just adding to the poor perception of the overall conversation whilst at the same time devaluing the company and the service. They were buying anyway, so whether they think I've done them a special deal or not is irrelevant. I may say, 'The price is £75 but, with your discount it's only £50'. Nobody mentioned a discount until then. I'm just giving them £25 because others are getting it, I'm allowed to, and because it feels good and guarantees the sale. They would have happily bought at £75. Everyone is doing it around me in the contact centre, so I will, too.

Imagine I'm a new mobile phone assistant when a customer comes into the shop and complains about their recent bill. I could go through their bill and point out their foreign and premium calls and their overuse of data. I won't of course, because that will take time, and is essentially blaming them for their own overuse, which is too complex and challenging, and I like selling new handsets, so I will probably make up some bull about the head office increasing tariffs without warning (and if that were true, I should be able to defend that action as it is almost certainly in the terms and conditions the customer originally agreed with). Instead, I say something like this: "Don't you worry, let me see what I can do.' I will let you have a discount, adjust your tariff still lower, even though you didn't ask me too, be happy that I have kept a customer, and not care less that the customer goes away believing, or disbelieving me about the company's 'unfair' decisions to increase tariff costs that I strangely disagree with, even though they are paying me. The truth is that I have seen my manager do the same, my colleagues do something similar, because targeting and product incentives take precedence over delivering great service and supporting my company to make it a profitable enterprise.

This lack of understanding of the importance of service and retention, destroys loyalty. Your own people are chipping away at the loyalty wall so that it eventually becomes unstable and makes it far more likely that the customer will eventually leave. If I believe I am selling a commodity, then I should be selling the commodity on the value it represents to each customer. If I don't then I will always undersell it, discount it, undervalue it, not be able to put the price up, etc, because I can't see the value myself - or be skilled at getting that value across to the customer effectively.

3. The third and most obvious reason, is that this way of selling, the 'like me' lie, is so culturally endemic that I can't help but start using it, to the extent that large groups of people will be using these statements completely unconsciously, sometimes in hundreds of conversations every day. The results in terms of conversion rate (percentage of sales against call numbers) may look great, but there's a real chance that I am feeding annoying, expensive to service, and price conscious customers into my system when I really want them to be quick, loyal, satisfied and profitable. The customers who say, 'I was told that I could call back after 18

months and ask for another discount... so that's what I'm doing.' These are the customers we are nurturing. We are setting ourselves up for problems if we keep on kicking the can of 'full price', or 'higher prices' or 'price increases' down the road. At some point we must charge that, or what's the point in having it at all?

Reputation of a brand is fragile. If word gets around, via thousands of customers, that you are a pushover when it comes to pricing and discounts then that reputation will take years to rebuild. The brand will always be trading at a false level of turnover because the sales will be made through lies or unconscious disloyalty. One day, those behaviours will reach a level where it's hard, or impossible, to reverse the trend.

Imagine you were a business buying advertising and you booked an advertisement with me over the phone, to appear on the web or in a magazine or newspaper, to help you sell something. And I made a mistake when taking down or receiving the advert and it was printed or shown incorrectly. You would phone up to complain. If you got through to me, would I admit that it was my mistake? Much easier to say it was a production error and re-run the ad. That's a total lie. I should admit my mistake, apologise, and offer a refund as well as a free advert. You would appreciate the honesty, possibly, and perhaps be more likely to advertise in the future. As an advertiser I don't care at all where the problem happened and whatever your explanation, I am given the impression of a useless set of production individuals, a misleading salesperson, a badly administrated company, and this contributes to a feeling of 'won't use them again'.

The other problem is that sometimes our managers and companies are *asking* us to do this. 'Look, results are poor, so use any and all means, to give us better results. Tell them it was a production error and offer to rerun the advert at a discount.' They would never say, 'use any means that don't damage our integrity, to keep the customer happy like compensating them for a useless advert.' They are accepting that we will be using occasional untruths and slightly dodgy language to persuade and cajole customers into buying. The idea of lowering prices until someone says yes, is also perceived as harmless, whereas, over the medium to long term this is devaluing the products and services, by locking in low quality/unprofitable business. Targets and an obsession with hitting them to trigger commission and bonuses contributes to this motivation too.

This is also about bias. I hear someone on the telephone who is old, so I feel sorry for them, irrationally, and this gives me a nudge to try and do something for them, through a patronising, sympathetic tone. Or I assume every person I speak to is concerned about price, so that's what I stick on, because I would be concerned about it as well, so my bias is to offer blanket discounts. I hear accents, and assume someone is poorly educated, or I assume someone is wealthy, they have an annoyed partner, or any number of invisible biases that populate my mind but are rooted in nothing but my own assumptions. I can then blame the customer's feelings about the value of my company on a system rather than take responsibility and explain to my manager that 'I had no choice,' but to give the customer what they wanted, even though it places us at a disadvantage; 'Well, at least we kept the customer'. Yes, but at what cost?

Companies also say, 'Isn't the customer always right?' We would say that the customer has plenty of rights. The customer cannot be blamed for what they are unaware of or have not had explained to them. They also don't have the right to be rude or unreasonable. They don't need to raise their voices and your staff don't need to listen to abusive language. At the same time, we must see the situation for what it is: customer's buy. They are the ultimate paymaster. Whilst they may not be right due to ignorance or rudeness or tone, they are important and we need the skills to handle them in a way that benefits both sides.

Chapter 2: Disloyal Bonding on the Phone (Contact Centres and Major Brands)

1.3 million people work in contact centres in the UK – 4% of the entire workforce.
Thisismoney.co.uk, July 2020

Acquiring a new customer costs 5–25 times more than keeping an existing customer.
Harvard Business Review

Most contact centres for large organisations have three departments. Sales or New Business, where new customers join or buy for the first time, Retention, where customers are kept and renewed, and then variations on Customer Service dealing with administrative stuff and technical queries. Of course, new business may come directly from the internet or from retail outlets or even through the post. Some businesses have regular customer interactions yet operate with no retention team or strategy at all, and all advisors receive all manner of calls.

It's a reality that, in regulated markets, if we want decent deals as consumers, then at some point we need to make calls to companies to either get a better deal than we already have, move to a lower cost option, or to be made to feel okay about our current deal. I'm thinking in particular about annual payments for insurances, phone contracts, energy contracts, water, broadband and any subscription service that we buy from a commercial company. (Sadly, local government subscriptions like Council Tax are not usually negotiable!) We may also be re-negotiating a better mortgage deal or asking for a loan or another financial service, which is something we compare, like credit cards, or pensions, or investments. Financial services of course, are far more regulated, and the language chosen needs to be more considered carefully to make sure a sale is compliant and not fraudulent. That said, many financial services will have disloyal bonding teams; they just don't realise it.

I might have to ask for a new mortgage, and my mortgage broker will happily curse the slowness and the draconian rules of the lenders he is getting me quotes from, not realising that this puts me off getting a mortgage from those lenders. Having said that, am I that bothered if I end up paying a lower mortgage? Am I subscribing to the game rather than challenging it?

When we make these calls, each time we are not only asked to assess the value of the product or service, but we are also asked to judge the level of service we have received. This is called NPS or Net Promoter Score. 'How likely are you to recommend us to others?' We then score the company out of 10 and this is now a vital metric, pored over by analysts. The idea is simple, if you score 9 or 10, you are an advocate – highly likely to recommend. If you score 8 or 7 you're neutral, and anything less, you are an active detractor of that brand. Sadly, NPS is a misused and misleading metric which we would advise against taking too seriously, for many reasons, which we have talked about on our podcasts, in articles and in other media. Essentially, NPS is measuring the wrong thing

– a skewed view. Nevertheless, it is still the current default metric for many. The score you give the advisor is very important to the brand. You would think that the score you give, would be your honest assessment. These days no one is taking any chances though. It's apparently okay to say, 'You'll receive a survey after this call, it scores me out of 10, and in case you were wondering, 9s and 10s are great!' So, you're begging them for a 9 or 10. They may have thought you were pretty average, but you still win the award! What does it matter to them if they've been given what they want? They'll score you high because you've asked, not because they've seriously judged your service to be outstanding. Also, how seriously can we really take a hastily filled out survey? Consumer's may hurry through them to save time rather than really seriously consider how they were served.

NPS is ultimately subjective, and for us, a selfish metric. It feeds Disloyal Bonding. If you call your insurance company and say that your renewal premium is too high, and they lower it, you will score them highly because they have given you what you want. Similarly, if you made an unreasonable demand to halve your premium which they could not match, you would score them low, regardless of how well they defended their brand and their pricing. You can see that this assessment of service quality is far too subjective and is often measuring the wrong thing, and yet businesses hang their strategies around this data as if it is the Holy Grail of business metrics. We know people who receive big bonuses because their NPS has increased. If they achieved that through Disloyal Bonding, then what are they being paid for? To totally screw up their business? Where's the increased revenue the business was looking for? That's just been paid that out in bonuses to executives who, probably unwittingly, are driving disloyal behaviours through the brand, but the effects of it won't be realised until long after they're gone and are enjoying their luxurious retirement. They will make speeches to their low paid staff saying, 'You've achieved these record figures, record NPS, record customer acquisition and retention, thanks so much for your hard work.' Then pocket a huge wedge and don't worry about 'how' they did it, because that will be someone else's mess to clear up. A selfish metric.

Over the last ten years we've trained thousands of people in contact centres all over the World. Culturally, different places have different levels of Disloyal Bonding. In India, there was no conscious disloyalty at all. However, there was a bias towards price. When the customer said 'Hmm that's a bit high' the tendency was to discount or look for something of a lower price, rather than sell and resell the value. Culturally, there was no issue with this – because that's how business is largely done on the subcontinent. There is a basis there that says, 'everything is negotiable'. We spent a considerable amount of time explaining that when someone discounts too quickly, that also can infer that the price was too high in the first place. They agreed that it probably was, but that was okay, everyone expected that! It's a different perspective, like an unspoken, pre-agreed game.

To see how this plays out, for example, I am booking a hotel room for a stay in New York, and the hotel I have chosen means that the advisor says, 'It's 300 dollars per night.'. I consider this, and my knee jerk reaction is 'That's a bit high.' At this point, there are several options. They can explain the quality of the room, hotel, location and justify the value, and that may work, whilst I consider if it's worth it. They can apply a discount 'Actually, I can do that one for $275.' So, that sounds better, but it also means that the $300 was actually ripping me off in the first place, doesn't it? And I'm not staying for an additional night, so that discount is a net loss. Why didn't you offer $275 immediately? And thirdly, and most common in our work in India, the tendency was to immediately look for a lower cost hotel altogether. 'You think that 300 dollars is too high? Fair enough, let me look for something at a lower price.'

This isn't disloyalty, but it is assuming that the original quote was poor value from the customer's point of view, when on further consideration, it may very well have been great value that they haven't yet fully appreciated, and by not supporting that, I have devalued the service, the hotel, and possibly the booking company, too. It suddenly looks like you will take any booking at all, rather than book me what I want, at a price that delivers me the right level of value, for me. Why not take the time to find out what that is?

In the United States, in the main, the contact centres we have worked with there, are populated by enthusiastic people who would not dream of running down their own company or de-valuing their products or services (certainly to customers). We're not saying it doesn't happen, but our instinct and experience of working there is that it happens less. Working in Europe, there are varying types of this behaviour, but still much less than we get in the UK. We believe this is a very British habit. Perhaps our levels of service are worse? So much so that we require some lies to help us survive. How sad if that's true. When we have heard it abroad it has been much more conscious: a disgruntled employee; someone leaving and going elsewhere, someone being disciplined, maybe.

One of the most common habits in any contact centres is long pauses, caused by slow systems. We blame our systems for so many things that make our service bad. 'It's slow.' 'It's crashed.' 'For some reason it won't let me.' as if some gremlin inside the computer is short-circuiting the system just to annoy you. 'Sorry, my system is very slow today. Don't blame me,' is what we're saying, for the slow way in which you are being served. Of course, what we're also saying is, 'This company is too tight-fisted to invest in decent IT, so the fat cats at the top are earning fortunes from your money, whilst we, the minions have to cope with outdated hardware and software, and have to make up some bull to mollify you...' The customer may not think that of us, yet, but it's feeble when you think about it. If the system really is slow, why can't we empower our people to make decisions that will bypass the system and maintain a high service level? We know, mostly, what the outcomes are likely to be for customers, so why can't we rely on the integrity of a conversation to create that outcome, and then work out the slow IT later, or get someone else to load it on the system?

Instead, we expect customers to sit in silence whilst we watch the whirring of the machine, and sometimes those silences are many minutes long. 'Can I put you on hold?' You go and get a coffee, grab a snack, the customer thinks you're sitting there slapping your computer trying to get it working, but you're using this regular occurrence, the apparent, slowness of the system, to have a short break. To add insult to injury, customers have to spend thirty-five minutes on a call that should take fifteen. And ten minutes of that is spent going through endless red tape, the terms and conditions at the end of the call that they honestly couldn't give a damn about, but your compliance people make you read it out because they're scared of falling foul of their marketplace rules and the government financial authority inspectors.

Instead of explaining the legal reasons why it's important for you to hear certain things we say 'I'm sorry I have to read this out, why don't you put the kettle on...' or 'I know this is annoying but, this is the terms and conditions for your protection and ours, shouldn't take too long...'. So, we've devalued the company through blaming the slow system, devalued the price by not selling the value and being useless at negotiation, and we've now shown that our compliance people are such wimps that they can't take a recording of you saying 'Yes, okay I'll have that', as confirmation that you truly understand what you have bought. The idea that reading out the terms and conditions will actually go into your brain in a way that makes you understand them is laughable; you just want it over and will say yes to just about anything to speed things up.

Contact centre advisors, when we question them about the ten minutes of t's and c's, often say 'You think these are too long? You should have seen what they used to be like!' Are you joking? You mean your poor customers were forced to listen to fifteen or twenty minutes of meaningless verbiage to placate a worried compliance or quality executive? Surely it cannot be beyond the wit of mankind to create a simple way of doing this, and sending you the dull but necessary compliance wording? 'People don't read it if we send it.' Right, so why say it as well, then? They've made that choice; send them the documentation and then it's up to them?

All the way through the call, we are unconsciously making you feel more negative about the company you are potentially buying from, but then, when it couldn't get any worse, the really bad Disloyal Bonding sets in. You say, 'Wow, that price is a bit high!' And we say, 'Yes, it is a bit, it's one of our more expensive packages?' And this shows how essential language is. To some people, *expensive* means high priced and might suggest higher quality, and to others, expensive means 'not worth the money you're paying'. We've just described this as an expensive package so if that means it's not worth the money to you, why should you want to buy it, now?

Cheap and *expensive* are subjective terms that mean different things to different people. As a contact centre advisor, if you think that what you are selling is *expensive*, then if you are telling that to loads of people, you are saying to all of them, 'I really don't think it's worth the money'. If you're *not* saying it, using actual language, then your tone will certainly be telling the customers, or a high percentage of them, what you really feel.

You'll wonder why your results aren't that good, or why the wins that you do get, are lower profit makers. At the same time, the advisor will say, 'let me find you a cheaper solution.' To some, *cheap* means lower cost but, to many, cheap means poor quality. Most customers don't want a cheap deal. They want a deal that gives them what they want, for a bit less. Or one that they will value more.

As consumers we know that companies want to make money, we don't want that money to be excessive, we certainly don't want to feel we are being ripped off, but that is what Disloyal Bonding does, it makes us believe that you're making way more from me, and many others, than you probably should.

'Yes, that's an expensive package'…'Yes, you're paying too much,'…'Yes, that price has leapt up after the introductory period, hasn't it?' You are agreeing that your company is charging too much! You shouldn't do that! Should you? You want to make money. They're not friends. You don't have to mollify them. All you need to do is sell them the value of your product. If they think you're expensive, whatever their definition of that is, that's their opinion. It doesn't mean it's right. Prove the value and they may think, on reflection that you're pretty reasonable. What they don't need is for you to make them believe the company is trying to rip them off, but that luckily, they've got through to you, and together, bonded as fellow humans for a few minutes, both sides will conspire to create something special that is disadvantageous to the company, but very advantageous to advisor and customer. This is a silly, and deceptive game. Both sides are making fools of themselves.

We were once sitting in a contact centre clicking from call to call, listening to the interactions. Everywhere there were advisors using Disloyal Bonding to placate a customer. It was dull, very low level, and even when it was effective, keeping or pleasing a customer who went along with the disloyalty and thanked the operator for doing something 'special' for them, it was still a bit embarrassing that this large company had had to resort to this behaviour to succeed. None of the solutions were that special, either.

Suddenly, we hit upon a call where the customer was really questioning the integrity of the brand.

'I've been with you for eighteen years, and you stick the prices up every year and now, I've had enough! New customers get better deals, there's no reward for loyalty and you're ripping off your customers!'

I was fully expecting the advisor to agree and use Disloyal Bonding to bond with the customer and placate him. But no. This chap dug in. 'No sir, that is not the case. We are a major brand, and we don't rip people off. Our price increases are in line with the enhanced benefits you've been given in your letter and in your policy. If you're not happy with them then you can call us, as you have, to adjust. When you were a new customer, you would probably have joined with an introductory offer, as most did. Now most of our customer base stay with us on standard prices, because they appreciate the value we offer, we have many customers like you, and we work to help you realise that we value that relationship and the service we can offer you.'

Wow. This was amazing. He was earning exactly the same as his colleagues. His results may well have been average or below average. Yet, he was defending the business better than anyone. This is so very rare I'm afraid. Would this chap be rewarded for his loyalty? Would he be applauded for the way he defended and talked the customer around? Even if the customer cancelled, he would still have left the call believing that the operator, and maybe the company, stood for something. That contribution is huge, that's a great reason to give this person a bonus, unlike so many of his colleagues.

5% retention increase → 25%-90% profit increase

Increasing customer retention by 5% boosts profits by 25%–90% **Harvard Business Review**

Contact centres thrive on structure and habit – and copying what other people do. We once worked in a contact centre where everyone gave away the pence. 'That's £493.72, tell you what, we'll take off the pence…'. Really? We worked out that at an average of fifty pence per call they were giving away over £300k every year! A habit that everyone copied.

The biggest change since the start of the pandemic has been the rise of enforced homeworking. This trend has simply sped up and now thousands work from home, connected via the internet. Managers have had to learn to manage their people remotely, and this isn't easy. The loneliness for many people of working from home, means that you only have yourself to monitor how well you're doing. Calls can still be recorded, but there's still a slight feeling of *I can do what I want*. The environment is different from a supervised office and that disconnection could well be a breeding ground for people trying out underhand techniques to earn a bit of commission. There's also the distraction of people coming around, deliveries, children, animals and school runs to negotiate. These take on a high priority and taking or making some calls, suddenly looks dull by comparison. To be self-motivated at home is not easy for everyone. In the Year 2000, around 3 million people in the UK worked from home. In 2021, the number had more than doubled to 8.4 million (ONS) – sped up because of the pandemic. That's more than 10 percent of the entire UK population working from home, with no need to commute, and with a huge need to create an effective work strategy.

Increase in homeworkers in the UK

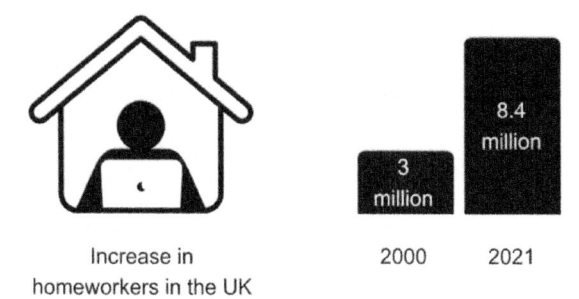

	2000	2021
	3 million	8.4 million

The number of homeworkers in the UK increased from 3 million in 2000, to 8.4 million in 2021. **ONS**

Employers have had to get used to the idea and are still wondering what to do with their large but unused premises in city centres. We trained thousands remotely on Zoom and had to experience myriad home interior designs in the background. Luckily, this worked well. But there's still a reluctance to turn on the camera, to be seen, to speak, to engage - almost a fear of being found out. Managers need to be very clear on their expectations of homeworkers, and that Disloyal Bonding is not a tactic that will be tolerated simply because someone is not present in the physical sense.

    As trainers, our lives are spent creating sales and service models that avoid Disloyal Bonding and yet people can't resist. They really believe that this easy lie, that we are actually working for you the customer, with you the customer, as friends, is a valid, sound and commendable sales technique.

Chapter 3: Disloyal Bonding in Face-to-Face Selling

UK is suffering a shortage of skilled B2B salespeople
Business Money, 10th March 2021

Online retail sales (as a proportion of all retail sales) increased from 19.8% in Feb 2020 to 27.9% in July 2021
ONS

Salespeople spend 66% of their day on administrative tasks.
Hubspot

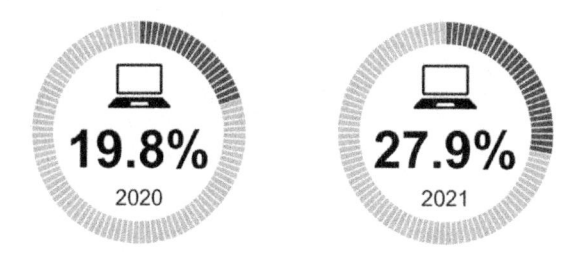

The percentage of online retail sales increased
from 19.8% in 2020 to 27.9% in 2021(ONS)

In the 21st century, most of us will only experience face to face selling in retail situations, buying cars or other major purchases, or when we invite salespeople to our homes for building work, double glazing, or other improvements. In truth, the internet has been slowly killing retail for years and the pandemic has merely sped that up. Many of us now buy things like groceries, clothes, shoes, wine, beer, perfumes, IT, furniture, travel and so many other products and services through the click of a mouse. The idea of going somewhere to speak to a human being, face to face, is slowly disappearing, or appears outdated. Another reason for this demise is that sometimes the human-to-human interactions we experience are so poor, so low level, that we are unsurprised, entirely, that certain products and services are better bought online, where we can select in peace and not be subject to the abject behaviours of poorly paid assistants, who rarely know enough or possess enough skill to truly help us.

Forty years ago, professional retailers were everywhere. Pre-internet, you needed to be so good that people came back to you again and again. Shops were manned by positive, trained and engaged people who made the process a pleasure. They also made money because they were skilled in cross-selling and upselling. If you bought a suit, they would naturally sell ties, cufflinks, shoes, shirts etc. There was an assumption that it wasn't just about the sale that day, but a series of sales over many years. Surely, that's how you build a retail business?

Bob writes: Not that long ago, in a previous job, I was given a 'car allowance' rather than a company car. I was looking forward to experiencing the pleasure of buying a new car. I went to a number of leading brands, walked into the showrooms with an amount to spend in my pocket and was quite willing to be sold a new car. It would be inappropriate to mention brand names… (they were all German!) but some ignored me, some patronised me, some didn't get back to me and one, which was briefly my favoured brand, was so useless that I swore never to buy from that brand again. The person I engaged with didn't sell it to me. He wanted me to select, and this is a very lazy way of selling. You think you're doing me a favour, but this is a big purchase. Help me. Sell it to me properly and make me feel good about it, please.

Let's consider the importance of that. Automotive brands survive on the idea, and it was only an idea, that you would buy from them, every few years. If the service was outstanding every time then the likelihood of that was much higher. If your service was shocking, so surprisingly poor that I cannot believe it for a major brand, then a) I won't buy now b) and I am very unlikely to buy in the future, plus c) I'm going to tell everyone about it. The major brand, incidentally, makes an assumption that their dealer partners will offer a service level that is so high that this locks in the customer's devotion to the brand. If they actually knew that people were offering a below average level of service to people who want to buy, they would seriously consider the value of that relationship and perhaps allow more customers to buy direct. That dealership level of poor engagement is effectively disloyal. That's devaluing the car (when I want to value it highly and be excited by the act of buying it) to a point where my post-purchase negative feelings, will continue to damage the brand still further.

Jeremy writes: I became very alienated by extended warranty packages. Having been bitten in the past, I soon developed an antipathy for them at a time when they were still the norm and sold strongly.

I needed to replace my laptop and, having had too many bugs with my PC in the past was seriously keen to explore shifting to a Mac. I drove to a Retail Park thirty miles away that had a couple of suitable chain outlets. I would be returning with a new computer, come what may.

For once, I actually wanted to be nobbled early by a sales assistant. I wanted to learn more about Macs – what their limitations were, what they were less good at – before opting for a Mac or another PC. I told this to a lad who approached me, eagerly anticipating the technical advice.

"Well, the first thing you need to know about a Mac", He said, "is they're expensive to fix if they 'go wrong'. So, you need a good extended warranty package."

"That's it," I said, "I'm off." "I am spending a fair bit of cash on a new computer today – but not here." I went next door and bought a PC. (I now have Macs.) Three years later, the second retailer I visited swallowed up the first.

Some retailers, like Apple, put product and price integrity at the heart of what they do. You would never hear an Apple employee having a negative opinion at the poorness of a product, its expense, its build quality, the way they're employed, their training, their manager. If they did have a complaint, then the last person they would air it to is a customer. Face to face their principles are simple and effective. First name terms for everyone. Explain what you're doing. Be informative, enthusiastic, and grateful for the sale. Don't worry about the prices because there's rarely a discount anyway, and they're the best products in the category. So, if the customer wants it, they'll buy. Just make them feel good about it. Make them feel good about coming into the Apple store. Trying the products, being present but not in their face, being honest about what you know and what you don't. It sounds so simple, doesn't it? Looking back at this paragraph, the face-to-face way to sell is simply being friendly, honest, believe in the quality for the price you are selling at and help customers feel good about the brand and your products - whether they buy or not! That's retail as it should be.

Net Promoter Score (NPS) is used as a poor measure by many automotive brands, who don't realise that if I buy a car that I love and the service is poor or average, then I'm quite likely to score the service highly, only because I'm pleased with the car and not because the service was any good. The salesperson could even have bad mouthed the brand 'they used to offer spare wheels with every car, but now, none of our cars have them.' in a disloyal fashion, and yet if I'm happy with the car I may well rate you highly. Then brands wonder why they don't sell so many cars, why people don't change them more often, why they have large car parks full of unsold inventory, and then need to discount heavily to shift them, and thus kill profitability? These un-checked actions have big consequences when the average sale is £30-£40k, and the margin, wafer thin as it is, is split between salesperson, dealer, and the brand.

Double glazing salespeople are also well known for their tricks. The fact they're in your house already means they're half-way, or more, towards a sale. Yet rather than sell you a high-quality glazing solution for £5k, they float prices in front of you, then play the ludicrous game of pretending to call a manager to get permission for an additional discount. This means there's no price integrity, and this behaviour, designed to con you into thinking you're getting a great deal, actually devalues the double glazing because it clearly was never worth £5k in the first place. This means the sales pitch is more about 'music man' which is effectively: 'Let me entertain you, we'll have a bit of fun and then enjoy the silly and immature game where I lose any integrity whilst striking a deal'.

Travel agents also have disloyal traits. Customers sit down in front of the in-store screens and the agent helps them search and book. Immediately it starts. The customer will be looking at online lists of holidays with a vast price range. The agent immediately ignores any holiday with a price which they feel is beyond the customer's means. They'll point at the screen. 'That one's a bit expensive', they opine. To whom? It's not their money? My partner likes 5-star luxury and pushing the boat out. But because I'm scruffier than usual this weekend, you've decided to offer me a budget option and devalue the higher cost options. They don't even know they're doing it. Any travel brand could be selling holidays for much higher amounts, but because their people disloyally push the lower cost options, the customer is either mis-sold (complaints time) or doesn't buy at all and is forced online or to a better service option which may cost more, but gives them the quality they want, at a price level they are happy with.

Any purchase like a holiday, which has a gap between the purchase and the delivery, must consider that the longer that gap and the higher the amount of money involved, the more likely the customer is to get cold feet or feel they've made an error. Selling the right thing at the right time in the right way is actually more important than discounting until the person says 'yes'.

So many retailers and face to face salespeople will throw opportunities away because a customer decides for whatever reason, not to buy. Rather than using it as a chance to set up a sale for the future, they immediately moving away or leave the conversation. When the customer has said 'maybe next year' then the salesperson should lock in the commitment and make them feel good about that future purchase. Instead, the salesperson moves on quickly to a better immediate prospect and demonstrates that the apparent interest they had, was just to make the customer buy something there and then.

In Business-to-Business sales, you would imagine this happens a little less. But it's still there. Account Management is the big thing, having clients who buy more and more, year on year. The Account Manager, poorly trained, will never remind their client why they like buying from the Account Manager's company. They will forget to sell the company entirely and leave it wide open for competitors to steal business. They assume their friendliness and their ability to take an order is enough, when it isn't.

Salespeople sit in meetings with customers, drinking poor quality coffee, pretending to be friends. They're desperate to sell something because they're having a bad month. Under pressure, they then play games in their own mind. If they let this client have a bigger discount, a one off, then they only need to sell something to someone else for a bit more, to make up for it. Will the client or their boss recognise that they've done this? Devalued the business and the relationship?

In sales many call their clients to 'have a chat' but of course they really want to sell them something. So they go through the charade that they're friends and then they slip in an offer, and now the customer feels obliged to consider it because they've been chatting about unrelated, nicer things for so long. It's an underhand tactic, but is it? Business to Business (B2B) clients can always look elsewhere. And remember, they know what it's like to have to hit a sales target, too.

In B2B advertising sales, Disloyal Bonding is endemic. One of our training clients once said that over the years the cost of his business magazine advertising had gone down hugely. The magazine salespeople seemed too scared to increase their prices. They were constantly discounting and offering him 'late space'. He recently decided to make things easy for them and said, 'Okay, I want a price for 12 months. If I book every week, what's the price?' Two weeks later he was still waiting. His rates were already rock bottom for ad hoc adverts. The magazine didn't want to give him any further discount but were afraid to say so. Instead, they waited and hoped his question would go away. They were almost admitting that any price, wasn't really worth it, and that his approach to commit was actually potentially more damaging than carrying on as before. When we spoke to the magazine, they were mortified that this request would set a precedent where all their major advertisers were stuck on low rates and this would kill the business. They assumed that they would always do better calling from week to week and 'pretending' to have a special offer.

Business magazines and website are only aimed at people in that industry. If you are selling to the industry, how else are you going to reach them? If anything, you should be paying more, because of the niche. Poor selling and account management over the years have dumbed down advertising to the point where the value of the audience is disregarded, and the advertising 'rate card', the full rates charged for the adverts, is considered to be a joke. Debasing and devaluing the product again. Why bother to publish advertising rates if nobody ever pays the full price?

We once had a project to book £500k worth of advertising with magazines and national newspapers. Our client asked us what sort of discounts he could expect? We reckoned a minimum of 40% - 50% off, and we were right. To him that meant he was actually able to buy 40% more advertising for his money – effectively £700k worth. We remember speaking to one leading newspaper and the price just plummeted, came down and down on every slight objection, and they had started low anyway! This is an industry that doesn't believe in it's rates.

Field sales people often sell uninteresting things to businesses. Their success is reliant on being enthusiastic. If you can do that, then you may well be okay, but if you're bored out of your mind then this will come across to customers. This means *acting as if* you believe this product is great for the duration of the meeting or conversation. If there is a problem, your disinterest will mean you're more likely to be disloyal and damage the account relationship because you just don't care that much. When your manager asks why an account was lost, then B2B makes it easy to say, 'They found it for less elsewhere', or 'Someone else won it,' rather than 'I lost it'. In truth your attitude to the client and your approach, is what probably lost you the account because someone else had a better attitude and approach, as well as a good price.

Lastly, in hospitality, the service levels are still so amazingly low that most of us would rather vote with our feet than say something. In catering, a complaint is actually a gift. But we avoid them, or blame someone else, and this is worse. Learn the soup of the day. Try the food you're selling. Be an expert and be polite. Don't begin by explaining the thirty-minute wait, and don't moan about your boss, the Chef, your head waiter, the food etc. We're not impressed.

Chapter 4: Disloyal Bonding in Face-to-Face Service

7% of Americans report that ineffective service is their number one customer service frustration.

12% of Americans rate their number one service frustration as "lack of speed."

72% of customers say that explaining their problems to multiple people is poor customer service.
Statista

The lines between sales and service are continually blurred. We've had brands ask us to deliver sales training to both sales and service people, and then ask us not to mention the words *sales* or *selling* to either, as if they are dirty words.

Walking into a well-known automotive brand the other day, Jeremy had barely gone past the entrance doors when he was witness to a disloyal bonding conversation. The customer was saying to an assistant; "I ordered it, it should be here and it's not - it's so frustrating!" Her response was; "The frustration you feel with Head Office is exactly the frustration that we feel, in store! They just can't seem to get it right, you have turned up here, the item is not here and, as I say, your frustration, is our frustration." It seemed that upping her volume and not reducing it as Jeremy approached, was a way of doing even more for the customer. As if she was also inferring, "I'm really happy for other customers to realise how bad things are, and to broadcast this around, so you can see how open and honest I'm being at the inefficiency of our company, and perhaps this will reduce your complaint and you'll still like us, well, me at least, and I may get some additional looks of sympathy?"

The man looked at her and pinched his eyes as if looking into the bright sun. Does this person really expect this customer to be sympathetic? 'Oh, you poor thing! Having to cope with this every day?' As if the customer would ever think that! "Right," he said. He turned on his heels and walked out. What are they wanting him to do? Never order from them, again? Did she really feel this is a good approach? How many people have witnessed this type of thing before?

Bob had a washing machine that malfunctioned. He thought of replacing it but was convinced, as it was still in warranty, to get an engineer out to fix it. After experiencing dreadful service to get the appointment and having to wait around for half a day before the guy showed up, the engineer arrived with the reassuring brand name stuck onto the side of his van. As luck would have it, the fix was swift and simple, meaning the washing machine was restored to full functioning glory in minutes. Bob was very pleased about this and expressed as much. He also mentioned the name of the brand, and how, he shouldn't have been surprised, at the ease of the fix, because it's a good brand.

Thirty minutes later, the engineer had filled Bob in on a) how the brand's washing machines were no way near the quality of their predecessors, b) how the brand had screwed him over in terms of his pay per visit, his expected fix time, and how he was poorly incentivised, c) how many appointments he attended which were unfixable, where the advisor who took the call could have established that with a couple of questions, and d) how he was looking forward to starting his new job in a few months with a more enlightened company.

Even when he had been through a positive service visit, Bob's opinion of this brand was altered forever by hearing about internal issues that should never be aired in front of customers.

Companies must accept all of the blame for this. It is an easy 'get out' to be reading this and thinking it is down to poor individual character, and perhaps we can lay it at the door of recruitment. 'Well, that's the person, isn't it?' It is far more about the culture, having a breeding ground of negative people. What has the company done or not done properly for years, to allow this attitude to pervade?

Bob was once moved from an office in London, which was reasonably accessible, to a new location ten miles away that wasn't, and was very costly to get to. He was furious about the lack of consultation and spent weeks moaning about this to his clients, and anyone who would listen. 'This bloody company, moving us to central London, where parking alone is £8 per day. Are they joking? – Anyway, let me try and sell you something…' It's unconscious, but he's clearly explaining how rubbish his company is to people who he wanted to sell to.

This behaviour also takes place in business to business, in other, different ways. Imagine I am selling something everyone needs, like insurance. If I am clever, I can present an image that states 'I am the expert. I have chosen to move to this insurance company, because it's the best bet right now in the marketplace, so that means you should buy from me.' Then when I move to another company in two years, I say the same thing, now slagging off the previous one: 'they were taking the mick, but this new one, this is the one for you.' It's a lie. They are simply moving the lie from brand to brand with no loyalty, trying to be above the brand they are selling for, in a way that projects *them* as being the thing you are really buying not the product or service. In a way it's a form of prostitution, lying about why you are moving to somewhere or someone new, because there may be little difference in product or service. Many people move simply because they're being offered more money and also because they've promised the new employer that they have the power to bring you, the customer, along with them. So, why talk about it in this way? Let your belief in the product do the talking, and be honest about your movement across companies because it benefits you more.

Garages are also guilty of this when they service your car. They will take the customer's side against any car brand in order to secure the work. They need to keep their workshop busy at a high rate of labour, with high-cost parts. It is not in their interest to be too loyal to a brand, just in case you pull up in one, cursing them. Bob's uses a mobile mechanic who prefers BMWs, but he's not over enthusiastic, in case Bob buys one and it suddenly dies on him. The other thing mechanics will do, when explaining how they haven't had time to finish fixing your car, is blame other customer's cars for the time it's taken to fix, rather than their ability to manage their time and fix their cars efficiently. 'Yes, that full service for the Jag came in and it's twelve cylinders, see? And a nightmare to get to the oil filter…' Again, do you want sympathy? You're actually saying, 'I'm such a bad/low skilled mechanic and so disorganised that I am not able to manage the workload we have, in a way that keeps our clients happy'.

Perhaps you're also saying, 'You wouldn't want to do this job would you? That's what you pay me for, so please sympathise with me, because we're all as bad as each other, the guys who fix your car, doing a job you can't, and please allow us some flexibility when it comes to getting around to fixing your Panda.' They're almost being disloyal to their own profession, which at some point we must assume was their choice?

The man from the Prologue took his car, a hybrid, into a garage because the battery wasn't charging. Remember the quote?

'Yeah, well those earlier models have got the old battery technology, haven't they, before it all changed?... oh, 2015? They were dreadful, you're lucky it's lasted this long really…'
Is the customer ever going to buy a hybrid car from that brand again? No way. In fact, this particular customer actually said to me 'That's it for me and this brand…'

Who is training these service managers to put down their own brand? Again, they think they are doing you a favour! They need to 'button their lip' and support the brand they're selling for. All cars have mechanical problems at some stage and sometimes they are costly, but if I've spent tens of thousands on a car, I really don't want an employee of that brand inferring that I have made a massive mistake. This will drive me away from that brand never to return.

I don't think tradespeople, or service people who work for large companies are ever trained in this. Many will make the wrong assumption that any employed person should be naturally grateful and loyal and keep internal problems to themselves. The internal failings of the company, are of course, not their responsibility, but the way they impact their ability to serve the customers is, and they need to understand that. Also, the way they are employed, their rotas, the way they are paid, is all private. The customer has little interest in that, and yet through sharing that, you may be trying to absolve yourself of the company's inability to get anything right, but again, it's just not necessary.

Some service people are very much against any idea that they are selling something. They want to deliver their service and be done with it. These days, because of the pandemic, no commercial business can afford to think this way. Everyone, every last person regardless of their position, is selling or helping to sell, *something*. This is a hard lesson. Some service people are natural, feel good, circumstantial salespeople. 'I'm literally up the ladder and I can see that this needs an upgrade?' Done deal. Others, because of a lack of incentive or confidence will never cross that line. A salesperson is less likely to put down the company than a service person, because the service person's culture is naturally looking for the fault rather than spotting the opportunity.

Chapter 5: Disloyal Bonding in Production, Pre-Meditated Disloyal Bonding...

Communication should travel via the shortest path necessary to get the job done, not through the 'chain of command. Any manager who attempts to enforce chain of command communication will soon find themselves working elsewhere.
Elon Musk, Tesla/SpaceX

When Bob was a student, he worked for a few months in a bullet factory. Well, it was actually a factory that made shotgun cartridges. The hours were long, and the pay was low. The job was to operate a large machine that quickly manufactured the cartridges. A shotgun cartridge is made of several bits, there's the case, some plastic wadding, the gun powder and the lead shot. The shot is either hundreds of tiny bearings for rabbits, targets or small game, or really large single bearings for lions, bears, baboons and elephants.

The job of the operator is to make sure the different bits all come together to make the cartridge, then box them up. When it's all working properly, the system means you can manufacture thousands of cartridges every day and then sell them all over the world. Once in a while, the supervisor, takes a cartridge, and fires it through a testing gun in a sound proofed room. This means that you test the velocity and the strength of the mix of gunpowder, against the speed and spread of the fired cartridge. It also makes sure you are making safe cartridges. The problem is that in between tests, you could, feasibly, be making sub-level cartridges. If the gunpowder amounts are a fraction too low, or too high, the wads are going in at a certain angle, or the shot dispenser is putting in too little, or too much shot. These issues would not be found out until the next test.

Bob would sit there, singing away (the machine was very loud) churning out cartridges all day long. Sometimeshel would notice one of the issues noted above, like the gunpowder dispenser was too low. He'd adjust and continue. Hundreds of cartridges could have been made with too much, or too little gunpowder. Here's the question, could he, the operator, have detected these issues earlier and adjusted? Yes, he probably could if he had been trained to do so. But he was not trained or empowered to do that. His job was to operate, the supervisors' job was to test, and nobody was interested in Bob's opinion as to whether or not he was producing consistent shot gun cartridges.

The effects of those mistakes could be minor; a mis-fired cartridge, you just eject and reload. They could also be major; if there's too much gunpowder then the minor explosion caused could potentially blind someone, or at least damage an expensive shotgun. Yet there was no empowerment. Nobody made Bob really think about keeping a closer eye, giving him clear parameters as to what was safe or what wasn't. That responsibility was the supervisors' alone. As a responsible person, Bob sometimes reflected on this, but the focus from the company was 'operate and produce, as there is huge demand' especially from a particular state in Africa which had a virulent baboon problem, by all accounts, and bought hundreds of thousands of cartridges. *Bob suspected he was arming them for a private war.*

Over the last twenty years we have heard stories about major manufacturers producing printing solutions, and mobile phones, where unempowered workers have allowed faulty products to enter the supply chain. The cost is ruinous. The new phone or photocopier arrives, the customer is excited about it, but 'oh dear, it doesn't work'. They call the supplier, the manufacturer, replacements, time, money, refunds and then the bad will that follows. A single faulty phone or photocopier can cost thousands in hours and salaries to replace, and thousands more in the customer saying to other potential customers, 'you'll never believe this…'.

The people on the production line probably know which products are faulty. Why haven't they been trained, and encouraged to make sure these don't go out? That one discussion, session, could save you thousands, or millions in lawsuits, but you don't do it because you still operate in this strange hierarchy that somehow thinks employees at a lower level, are not employed to decide and some of the 'higher ups' don't trust their judgement.

This is the essence of the current malaise in all – especially UK – organisations, public and private. The effects in terms of poor productivity, inflexible systems and exorbitant costs of doing anything at all are enormous.

Without training, and empowerment, they are unconsciously, disloyally, sending out poor products on the brand's behalf. Unwittingly growing a bad reputation that is also costing money.

In other countries including Japan they use entirely different methods of production, and this would never happen. In Japan, Managers on production lines, work alongside the workers. Their job is to continually improve the system, so that products are made with fewer faults, greater speed, and efficiency and at a lower cost. In other countries production managers are somewhat divorced from the proceedings, 'make occasional forays into the production line from the 'management factory', messing things up, and then disappearing again.' (As John Seddon says.)[1]

There are many management philosophies that underpin how you run your business, but the danger of the hierarchy is that it stops people improving things. Elon Musk of Tesla has a rule where ANY employee, regardless of position can disregard hierarchy if they spot a problem, or a way to improve things. That is true empowerment which will ultimately speed up production and profits.

Thirty years ago, Bob knew someone who worked on a car production line, making the Mini. He told Bob that for each car he was allotted twelve minutes to completely install the wiring for all of the electrics. This time allowed two minutes for snags or problems. That's not masses of time. You could imagine that if there was a snag which you couldn't fix

---

[1] John Seddon – Management Thinker – Author of 'Freedom from Command and Control'.

completely, you would have no choice but to let that car move on to the next stage, which would mean it could, down the line, have a small but annoying fault for the new owner. Would you tell a manager? Knowing it would be unlikely to be picked up on, until it was sold? You wouldn't if you were unincentivized to do so, if your manager annoyed you, if you felt you were poorly paid, or put under too much pressure, etc. This is delivering Disloyal Bonding with a customer you have never spoken to and will never meet. It is almost Pre-Meditated Disloyal Bonding. By allowing shoddy goods to go on to be sold, you've shown the customer exactly what you really think of the company and how it is run. All the time you're getting away with it, means there's no incentive to stop either.

Chapter 6: Disloyal Bonding and the Strategic Lies of Head Offices

In 2017, 1/3rd of employees believed their leaders had a negative effect on company culture
Comparably.com

It's hard to believe, but large organisations will have Head Office locations that are completely infected with the Disloyal Bonding problem. This is because, over time, systems and workflows are created that never change. These build up time wasting processes, gaps in delivery that never get filled, and hiatuses become rife. Rather than sort these things out, executives sit in head office and get more and more frustrated - or accept lazily that something just doesn't work very well and, without realising it, then feed it back through the people to customers.

Bob writes: I recently bought a new fridge from a major national supplier. Replacing a fridge is a pain, because you need to wind down all the stuff in your old fridge, defrost the freezer, just in time for it all to be picked up. So, the timing of the handover is really essential. To make matters more complex, you are given a half day slot, in my case between

7am and 1pm, which meant I needed to get up at 6am, finish emptying the fridge and have the old one ready to go.

Come 7.30am and the entire work surface in the kitchen is covered in jars, milk cartons and the general contents of the fridge. I'm waiting. At 8.30am I get an email – 'sorry due to logistical reasons the new fridge cannot be delivered.' I was fuming. I had to turn the old one back on, move it back into position, put all the stuff back into it, with no idea when the new one was arriving. It was a Saturday. I couldn't get hold of anyone at the contact centre, so I ended up finding the CEO of the retailer on LinkedIn and sent him a strongly worded InMail which clearly defined the problem in no uncertain terms. I also cancelled my order and asked for a refund. I was so incensed I didn't want to give the company a penny of my money because their service level was so useless.

I got a response from the CEO's assistant a few days later, apologising and offering me a 10% discount to reinstate my order. I was still angry. It wasn't about the money; it was the inconvenience that wasn't being addressed. I wanted a proper apology. I wanted an acknowledgement that this situation was unacceptable and that they would be changing their shocking delivery policies. So, rather than apologising in a human way, this CEO was saying 'the failing of our system and the frustration caused to you and the inconvenience of having to do this all again, because of us, is only worth 10% of the cost of a new fridge'.

10% is a standard, 'this will do' discount. That doesn't make me feel any better. The letter was a standard letter, one they send out all the time and just changed the name. They are clearly making so much money the rest of the time, that the few hundred times this happens is still only worth a small concession. In other words, they just don't care. The Head Office of a major brand in the UK, didn't care about its customers, and worse, its complaining customers, above a 10% discount, roughly £50-£80.

In the UK, if we have a complaint that we air to a company and they handle it to our satisfaction, then we will tell, on average, five people about it. 'Well, they screwed up, but they handled it really well, to be fair, I was impressed...'

On the other hand, if our complaint is dealt with poorly and we get even more annoyed with the brand, on average we will tell twenty people. 400% more. 'Even after this massive hassle, they still couldn't get it right. What a useless company. Don't ever go near them!' Many people will have heard of this statistic, but not many will have really done the maths.

If we have a company that has a million customers, spending £500 per year then that's a turnover of £500,000,000. Or half a billion. Nice business. Let's be kind and say 5% complain about something. That's 50,000 complaints. And let's be really kind and say 10% of those are handled well, 5000 people happy with how they have been treated. They will tell five others, each, so 25,000 either think or have heard that the brand is pretty good. Now, you have 45,000 people, unhappy or at least dissatisfied with the outcome. If they tell twenty people each that's 900,000 people every year being told how bad the brand is. So 900k versus 25k, the balance is shifting heavily against this brand's reputation.

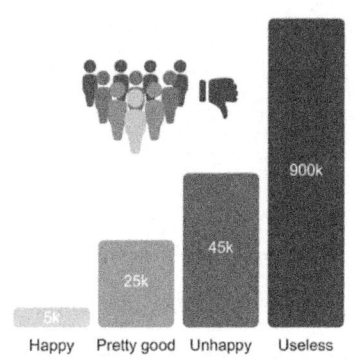

How people felt about the way their complaint was handled

This book is subtitled *Disloyal Bonding and Strategic Lies* – but equally could have been titled: *How Businesses Totally Screw Up*. On these sums it is showing you how easy it is, by being unconcerned about a complaint, for you to do just that. You want to grow your business? But right now, with 900,000 potential customers every year being told how rubbish you are, that's going to be harder than ever.

This is a Head Office strategy. Someone has sat down and said, 'Look, if we throw 10% at our complaints, or on average £50-£80, that should be enough to make most of them go away, it will also cut down on admin to deal with them.' Essentially, that idea, to give everyone 10%, is a) an amount you can afford and b) telling customers how unimportant they are to you.

The CEO who wrote to Bob may as well have written: 'Sorry about the hassle we've caused you, we are pretty bad at this, which is unsurprising when you look at what we pay people. Here's £50. Now please, would you just quietly go away?' At least, that is how he has been made to feel.

How many times have you stood on a station platform and heard this announcement 'The 08.17 train to London Bridge has been cancelled. We apologise for any inconvenience caused.' Again, somebody has decided, at a high level, that this announcement or variations of it, are enough. Look at the language. 'We need something that covers everything...' 'How about, we apologise for <u>any</u> inconvenience...' 'Perfect!'

You're on your way to a life changing interview, to meet the love of your life, to get to work on time, (when you've been warned about your lateness) to buy important gifts, food, clothes, to meet someone you have not seen for years for lunch, for a drink, for a coffee. It doesn't matter. Even if you're 'just' a commuter, well used to these cancellations, that apology comes nowhere near what is required. The cancellation is unacceptable. You are a modern train company, running relatively modern stock, on modern lines, using staff on rotas that you control, and yet you cannot avoid cancellations with less than ten minutes warning to your customers? You can introduce 'easy refund policies' thinking, that will placate some complainers, and hoping that many people won't bother. Again, you're hoping most will quietly go away. You actually know that the customer has little choice but to put up with your bad service anyway, so you've got them by the balls. You don't ever think that at any other time, weekends away, holidays, business trips, etc, the customer will do everything in their power to avoid relying on your hopeless services, which means you are stifling potential growth, and constantly damaging your reputation, by continual, unfeeling, corporate apologies.

Complaints is just one way that Head Offices show how they really feel about customers. How many of us, have been buying from a company for years, paying monthly or annual subscriptions, and then watched as new customers are rewarded with amazing offers that we have never had? Marketing Directors, their assistants, and a plethora of others have been paid very high salaries to sit in meetings and conclude, eventually, that the cost of acquiring new customers is so high, at least ten times more than the cost of holding on to a current customer, that the only way to attract new customers is to offer amazing or free introductory offers, which is treating with total contempt, your current, loyal customers.

We've sat in Retention departments, listening to so many customers say, 'I'm annoyed you're offering this to new customers, so I may as well cancel and re-join as a new customer.' Or 'There are no rewards for loyalty. It's not fair.' They're totally right, it isn't. You're relying on the fact that a large percentage have better things to do than check their outgoings or go onto comparison sites, and you hope that most won't notice an annual hike in prices and those that do, can be negotiated with. Only, when that previously loyal customer comes through, thinking, 'I've had enough of this.' instead of using integrity and honesty to explain your position, you actually allow or even encourage your employees to blame the company even more for its unfair practices because they haven't been trained to sell properly. 'Sorry the system generates the new prices, (it's not me – it's the company ripping you off) so, <u>let me see what I can do</u>, which will mollify you, even though you will ultimately feel worse about the company after this conversation.' I heard one call where the advisor said, 'It's not me that sets the prices.' Inferring that there is an unscrupulous criminal higher up that hikes prices up, as their whim takes them.

The price hikes for loyal, current customers are simply greed. Certain industries like insurance are clamping down on this, making it effectively illegal for an insurance company to increase prices after a year with no claims, beyond the prices that would be offered to new customers. Most agents in insurance contact centres will now have to sell insurance on the benefits of the policy, tailoring it to fit, and selling the company in a way they have never had to before. Many will not be able to do this effectively, so ingrained is Disloyal Bonding and poor-quality negotiation in what they do.

Finally, the leaders, CEOs, Chief Executives and Managing Directors of certain companies must shoulder some of the blame for encouraging these behaviours. *Bob Writes*: I once worked for an owner manager who ran a medium sized publishing house employing well over a hundred people. The magazines he published, at a time where the internet was about to slaughter his publications, were business mags, monthlies in the main, with a dwindling number of readers. The week I joined, I was asked to attend an exhibition in Birmingham, which meant a few nights away.

On the first day, the owner manager showed me a clunky, unexciting web site, which his readers could access, and request information about certain products that were listed there. The site had been developed at huge expense, to respond to the threat of the internet. What he hadn't realised, of course, was this site was, in effect, rendering all his product focused magazines redundant as advertising vehicles. If he was promoting a product search site that made it easy to find what you may be looking for, then why would you skim through a magazine?

As I watched him click around, I could see what a vanity project this company was for him. He had begun it when the UK was a different country, and he had profited as a result, because for a long time, these magazines were one of the only sources of product information for businesses. What he hadn't done was moved with the times. He had expanded, sure. He had employed more people, brought company cars, and hosted Christmas parties; his heart was certainly in the right place.

On the first night in Birmingham, we all attended a company dinner. He stood to speak in front of over fifty employees, who were all staying at the hotel. This was clearly a moment of pride for him, the owner, the employer, the hero of a company that turned over millions every year. He said, 'We had two objectives for this year, the first was to make a million pounds profit, and we didn't quite manage that...'

I really thought about this. They turned over £10 million plus. Paid everyone, paid all their costs, produced the magazines and websites and couldn't extract 10 per cent profit? I looked around at that group. Surely to make a million profit wasn't that hard? Sell more, cut some costs, sell some assets that weren't making any money? Throw out the magazines and go big on the internet and own that space? It all seemed pretty obvious. He was holding on to past glories and wouldn't hand over the business to people who would make the tough but necessary changes required.

That leadership style, or lack of, meant that cliques formed, those in favour of the good old days and those who wanted to drive change with the ultimate decision maker sitting firmly in the past. This meant the people he employed ranged from the decent and professional to the devious, self-serving and corrupt. Those negative people understood exactly what was happening and milked their gravy train for all it was worth. Which meant cutting unprofitable deals, selling their wares for less, year on year. Telling the MD what he wanted to hear rather than the truth; fighting against change, for fear of being found out for the second-rate salespeople some of them undoubtedly were. Their behaviours were entirely disloyal. If they had been honest with the owner, strategic in their thinking, closer to their customers, loyal to the company and expressed as much, then things might have turned out differently.

As the business contracted and struggled, they doggedly refused to do anything new and would cut worse and worse deals, devaluing their products - not all of them, of course, but enough to fatally wound the company.

David Ogilvy writes in his book, *Confessions of an Advertising Man* about the time when King Henry the Eighth was dying, and people believed that if anyone told the King the truth, they would be executed. Henry Denny stepped up to the plate. The King didn't decapitate him. For his bravery, the King was hugely grateful, as it gave him time to prepare, and he gave Denny a pair of gloves and a knighthood. Sir Henry Denny was an ancestor of Ogilivy. Clearly the world needs more people like him, who are prepared to speak the truth to power, and this 3rd tier business media company, owned by this single-minded ego, might have survived with a Denny or two. Having said that, the owner manager concerned, from his palatial office, was quite used to ignoring the realities of his situation and trying to trade on past successes. Egos are very fragile things, but for some they are everything. Hoping things will get better or will go back to how they used to be because one's ego can't stand to consider anything else, isn't much of a strategy.

The subject of company *values* also comes from the Head Office. Much attention is given to workshopping different values like 'trust' or 'innovation'. Promoted largely internally, the belief is that when a frontline employee has 'what the word *trust* means to our brand' explained to them, this will transform them magically into magnificent ambassadors for brand loyalty. The employee would much rather be paid more. If you take them to Telford for a night, and pay for a few drinks, a gala dinner sponsored by suppliers, and then present the new values in an amusing and upbeat way, then they may forget about how poorly they're paid. You've subjected them to a day or two of 'paid sabbatical', which means they'll go home thinking, 'What a great company, I'm going to project these values like there's no tomorrow...'. And you may get away with continuing to pay them as little as you do for a little while longer. Soon, the shine of the event wears off and the façade of investment will give way to the reality of feeling shafted. Then there's a knock at the moralistic door, and here she is: Mrs Disloyal Bonding. What about those values? The patronising, basic, obvious, and irrelevant values? What about them? On £20k per year my values are focused on my own survival.

The Head Office must be the guiding force for what is expected of all of their employees, and show, train, demonstrate through actions not words, what they expect and, if necessary, pay more to make sure it is demonstrated and delivered to customers.

Chapter 7: Disrupting the Disruptors – Your Heads of Disloyal Bonding & Strategic Lies and Your Wider Disloyal Bonding Cells

And since most organizations don't know who their influencers are or how information flows around, they are powerless to stop rumours or leverage their influencers for a counter-narrative.
Mark Powers, 'How to defeat corporate saboteurs in your workplace', LinkedIn, January 2020

When we begin a project with a large organisation, we listen to recorded customer interactions, observe retail conversations, accompany salespeople to meetings and run co-build workshops where salespeople and their managers can share their issues, challenges and opportunities with us. Frequently, we will meet a team leader of a top performing team of about fourteen people. This team is way ahead of others, in terms of conversion, Net Promoter Score and employee satisfaction. The team love their team leader and they perform <u>for</u> the team leader. The last thing they are working for is the company.

The truth is often that the team leader is letting them get away with anything and encouraging them to pursue any and all means to remain as top performers. We spot this pretty quickly and point out that if the team are retrained to sell with integrity, then the results are going to dip, or they may not be able to cope with the change. The truth is too much for certain companies. 'Oh no, we can't have that. Their contribution is so high we can't risk it dipping. Maybe we'll take them off the training.' Which means that you value the team's short term money generating performance, more than you value the long-term future of the business. It's a tricky balance.

If we can describe them as a disloyal cell, let's consider their effect on other teams. If their behaviour was confined to their own, immediate vicinity, that may mean it's not transferring or being noticed much by others, but when you're comparing their performance with people who are trying to sell with the long-term interests of customer and brand in mind, they will constantly see you reward these teams who indulge in the wrong behaviour. The manager of the 'good' team will soon get disgruntled. The advisors will start wondering if they can get away with what the 'disloyal cell' is doing and soon you have many more people devaluing your products service and brand, and damaging your reputation. You may not notice it for ages, watching other teams climb to the Number two and Number three spots, without realising you've now got three teams all doing and saying things to customers that are completely wrong, damaging and possibly dishonest.

Quite as scary is the realisation that you may have a Head of Disloyal Bonding. Is it you? Are you reading this book, thinking, 'Oh no, that's me! That's what I do!' If so, then make sure this book is worth the money by making some changes, right now. (The first thing to do is make sure everyone who can affect these behaviours is conscious of them.)

If it *isn't* you, but you sense the Head exists somewhere, you may be looking at your operational board, your Senior Managers, and thinking, who is great at driving conversion and revenue but whose profitability is a bit low? Who is great at new business but dreadful at renewals? Whose team is high performing, and has low staff turnover? Who has high staff turnover because they're trying to do things properly and yet someone has been lambasting them about performance? Who is responsible for your company hiring unethical people who are happy to lie, cheat or steal to hit a target? What are the criteria your HR team are using to get people in to do the job? Does your CEO 'glad hand' your Head of Disloyal Bonding because they make him or her look good to shareholders and ensure high bonuses are paid?

Many CEOs are in receipt of high salaries and will get an even higher bonus, based on certain criteria, for their two-three years of being in place for that brand. That bonus, which is where the money really is, may have very simple criteria. Revenue, profit (which can be achieved through cuts as well as growth) share price, new customer acquisition etc. From a CEO's perspective, they may well be a temporary shareholder or be given share options that vest just before they leave, but they're not an owner who is going to hang around, so the long-term reputation of the company can often run counter to their objectives. They may earn far more from large numbers of disloyal bonding teams, selling many low-level deals, than they would from the same teams selling smaller numbers of longer term, more profitable business. I realise that for some, this will be an uncomfortable truth. Some Senior execs are excellent and making a violent adjustment to a company's bottom line, and then moving on before the dust has settled. A bit unnerving and disloyal, isn't it?

Head Offices set annual and quarterly targets too. Jeremy used to work for one of the large directory companies selling advertising. The job was to renew current advertisers and get them to increase advert size, add colour etc, or take additional directories for new areas. The other job was to sell new adverts to new advertisers, mostly smaller businesses who were listed for free anyway, and there were a series of small sizes available from around £100, or even £55 per advert.

One quarter, the directive came down from Head Office. 'This quarter we are only interested in increasing the number of adverts. So, your commission will be paid on the number of adverts you sell to new advertisers.' The majority of the salespeople renewed their adverts and upsold to new directories, as many adverts as they could, and with what little time they had left, tried to win some new advertisers. Everyone did really well. One person just focused on selling to new advertisers only. She renewed the majority of her current list on a straight repeat of the year before, and then focused to sell hundreds of £55 adverts.

The team convened in a restaurant to be given their commission cheques at the start of the next quarter. One team member had increased the revenues of his accounts by 20%, this was current advertisers paying more, which they would continue to do for years. Because of how they were targeted, he earned about £1500 commission. The salesperson who focused on £55 adverts, (which had the lowest renewal value, 80% would never renew in Year 2) because of how they were targeted, earned £18,000 commission.

Effectively, all the money, and more, that they had generated was paid to them in commission. That directory brand, through this poorly considered head office directive, had put off potential advertisers by selling them rock bottom priced ads, that were never going to draw any response, rather than sell them something that might generate more business, and then make them more likely to renew the next year.

The salesperson with the large commission cheque had effectively lied to the new advertisers all day long in order to earn a silly amount of commission for doing something literally anyone could do, and yet they were congratulated by the Sales Manager because they had done what the Head Office had wanted. Suffice to say, that particular directory company no longer exists, it has been replaced by the internet, but also it died because its Head Office had no real, long-term strategy to compete and stay relevant. Gordon Gecko, in the film *Wall Street* said, 'Greed is Good'. Yes, usually for the greedy, rarely for the hungry, or those with some integrity.

It could be surmised that getting Jeremy and his colleagues to sell low value, high volume advertising in order to inflate the customer numbers shows how the impressions we make to the City, investors, company valuations and share prices, are closely linked to disloyal bonding practices. Asking salespeople, and they were good ones, not to sell with integrity, ultimately drove good salespeople to better companies.

Chapter 8: Recruiting for Integrity

Integrity begets trust. Without trust, people can't work together. Everything grinds to a halt.
CC Francis, Halcyon, Nov 2020

There was a time when salespeople, talented communicators, were vitally important, and relatively expensive to employ. Interviews often focused on past performance. 'You were selling advertising in this newspaper. What was your performance like, against your targets?' The salesperson then embarks on an entirely biased description of their successes. They are then asked that question about their biggest weaknesses, (where they usually choose something relatively harmless like excessive sarcasm or being a bit of a cynic) or what their current manager would say about them. 'They don't want to lose me'.

As potential employers, we consider their figures - How much money they have brought in. We may wonder how much activity has gone into achieving these figures. We can't really check that very easily, and most of us don't check anything. What we really cannot assess is actually how they achieved their sales successes. We don't know how they communicated with their customers; we don't know what sales skills they used to hit their targets or, indeed, what underhand methods, lies, discounts and creative bundles they pulled together. We don't know how much of that business would have happened anyway or how much of it was generated through active sales efforts. We don't know how many months they stopped selling to load the next month or how many times they held back orders for the next month, so they didn't go too far over target. What we cannot test is their integrity. What did they actually say to their customers; which skills did they use in order to persuade them?

Incidentally, I may be an employer or manager who doesn't have much integrity either. If they were to explain to me their methods, I might completely recognise what they have been doing and see little, or no problem with it. As a Sales Manager, I am also under pressure to hit targets, and because I am probably being managed poorly by my superiors, my belief is that they do not care how I and my team hit those targets, as long as we do.

Interviewing salespeople, can be a painful process. There are so many types: vulnerable narcissists and chancers; judgemental saints; twisters of basic truths; cliché dealers; old hands; young sparks; relationship junkies; systematic detail merchants; oversellers; conmen and conwomen; journeymen and journeywomen; outstanding candidates and a fair share of schmoozers.

Within all of these gregarious and surprisingly likeable types, you will find those who will fit your team well, and those who could never work with you or your team. This is often overlooked as a key criteria. Bob was once interviewed in a bar near Tower Bridge, drink in hand, standing up, telling stories. It wasn't really an interview as far as he was concerned. He thinks the guy with the power to appoint him was looking for someone who was socially confident, because that was a vital component of the job: selling to agencies and top brands, where, in those days, schmoosing was part of the deal. He got the guy laughing and bought him a beer. They had a strange negotiation and that was it. Great interview.

When you're sitting in an uninspiring office, interviewing someone, then their ability to fit in socially and business-wise is harder to assess. In the office they're on best behaviour, and you may not spot their character traits on the first meeting.

In many sales jobs you are given accounts, which is literally giving you sales and commission that you must manage. The management of these accounts is normally pretty straightforward, so, in giving this to you, the manager concerned may as well make sure it's someone that they and the clients will actually like, who could probably do a reasonable job. There may be an outstanding candidate who sadly doesn't realise how insufferable they are, which is why they don't always land the job. The Manager can't stand the thought of letting this person loose on the key accounts, which would adversely affect the clients, the team and everyone else, despite their clear qualification.

The Manager may meet a candidate with the gift of the gab. We've known male candidates talk about how they 'blag deals' and some female candidates admit they 'flirt it' on occasion. And yet, as a Sales Manager, who is going to help me hit target and guarantee my commission and keep others off my back? If I am ambitious, I may be looking for a Sales Director Role, a Commercial Director Board position further on down the line, so the employment of a couple of chancers, may give me exactly what I want. The gamble is, do I know the clients or marketplace well enough to judge whether these dodgy activities will be well received, ignored or complained about?

Brands need to be clear from the very top if they are truly serious about recruiting for integrity. What does that mean in terms of behavioural expectations? There is a world of difference between someone who 'takes an order' by discounting and someone who 'makes an order' through professional negotiation.

If the products or services are buyable through an enticing offer, that's great because that should mean you achieve some volume. Would these products and services ever be bought at full price? Ever? So, the offer culture, the discount scenario is actually a farce. 'The usual price is £120 but for you it's £70.' Truthfully the full price is £70 because that's the price point we reckon people will buy at, especially if they think that they're enjoying a £50 discount. Nobody buys at £120 and when they do, nobody can believe it.

My candidates then, would they have the capability and confidence to sell at full price? How would they do that? What skills, language or structures would they employ? If everything actually has a full price, that's the baseline, isn't it? The fact there are offers is a treat, but we should be convinced that what we are selling is worth the full price, first of all. If we don't believe that, this will be betrayed by our tone and how we come across. How can we test their ability to sell at full price or walk away, but have enough skill to leave the door open?

One of Bob's first jobs was selling 'machinery for sale' adverts into a business magazine in the timber market. People knew that the readers of the mag were in timber, and may be interested in these second-hand machines. A typical ad would be *Immense timber saw for sale, £8000 ono Tel...* This machine was worth up to £8k and they were spending £50 to advertise it to the only audience who could possibly be interested in buying it. As deadline day approached, we needed to 'fill space' with adverts. You would call previous advertisers.

> 'Have you sold your machine yet?'
> 'No, not yet. Had a bit of interest...'
> 'Shall we run the ad again?'
> 'I'm not sure I want to pay another £50.'
> 'Okay fair enough, I'll run it for £40?'

Think about that. How else are they going to sell their £8k machine? Why didn't we keep the price the same? Another £50, it's fair enough! I've also just taught the advertiser that next time they can call and get two weeks for £90. I am devaluing the ad when the value of it is exactly the same. I'm just mirroring behaviour of those around me, 'We need to fill the space with cheaper ads and it doesn't matter because we've made enough from the pre-booked ones, so just drop your price till the person says yes, and we'll fill it up.'

Integrity is okay until you're approaching your target or a fixed deadline, and then, somehow that integrity diminishes. Even if the customer's don't realise it explicitly they certainly feel it, and you know that your chances of increasing your prices any time soon are limited, because you are locking in a perception of value which means your business will function sub-optimally.

When recruiting, here's the test: 'When you're approaching the end of a month or quarter, what tactics do you use to persuade customers to buy when you really need them to?' That's the key question that will unearth each salesperson's integrity or awareness of it. They may just talk about persistently calling people or trying harder, but you may get some answers that you don't like here, which may be concerning, when what you're really assessing is, is this person trained to sell and manage their time properly.

The other difficulty is when you have a more senior manager leading the recruitment process, the candidates are appointed and assigned to a team. Regardless of their performance at interview, their sales behaviours will be influenced and adapted by their new team members, and if the team are a cell of Disloyal Bonding individuals, led by a manager who cares about nothing as long as targets are hit, then within days the newby will be using the same strategies. It's inevitable. Excellent, well-trained salespeople who believe in what they sell become warped by cynics who chip away at their enthusiasm and show them a short cut to success, which, when there are no direct repercussions, suddenly seems pretty tempting.

Some managers would say, 'Come on guys, if we sold everything with full integrity we'd sell less and be less successful.' I'd challenge that with, 'So you're happy to sell without integrity?' There are many, more harmless ways of applying discounts and offers, and we can train people to do it, but this must be underpinned with a belief that the products are worth the full price in the first place. A blagger can be useful and a flirter can get us some market share, but at what long term price?

We once interviewed someone who said, 'I'm going to be selling this with so much passion that...' We both thought the same, *journeyman* - someone who is essentially lazy but can turn it on from time to time with flashes of brilliance. We're suspicious of the word *passion*. You can say, 'He's really passionate': But to say, 'I have a passion for selling IT software', is clearly total rubbish. Personally, I have an enthusiasm for selling training contracts, my passions are my own private kingdom. This journeyman would blame anybody or anything except his own lack of effort for his poor results because the journeyman, the luxury player, will only turn it on when they really need to and often it's way too late, but just enough to keep them in gainful employment – clever. But remember, they're only loyal to themselves, never to you or the company.

Chapter 9: Training for Loyalty

We either win in a way that is fair and right, or we lose with our honour intact and face the consequences.
Elon Musk, Email to Tesla Salespeople who were going against the 'no negotiation, no discount' pricing policy

64% of companies expect to spend less than $10,000 on training their sales team this year.
Hubspot, 2021

Companies that train managers to manage their sales pipelines see 9% faster revenue growth.
Harvard Business Review

As we've already made clear, loyalty from employees is very tough to achieve. If we can do it, though, we can create profits and security. That's the reward for rooting out these disloyal behaviours. Some will think it is impossible to have a commercial organisation that doesn't have these disloyal behaviours somewhere. In any organisation of above a hundred employees with people doing varied tasks, to create consistent loyalty is vital, but really tough. How can you make sure that each person understands the importance of loyalty without it being constantly spelled out? And how many people are able to demonstrate that in front of customers in a positive way that makes them come across as persuasive and trustworthy?

What we are experiencing now, is a lack of enablement, through a broad naivety when it comes to understanding how businesses work. It's not that complex; it's just that so many don't believe it's really possible to get this right. It is a deeply held cynicism.

Apple is the best case, in point. They offer a premium product, desirable, higher priced, with accessories, and customers can be helped in a multichannel and omnichannel capacity, web, phone, retail, 24 hours per day, 365 days per year, etc. No Apple employee would consciously, or unconsciously talk their brand down. They wouldn't say, 'Oh yes, that Mac is the older one, which is not as good as the newer ones.' They would never say, 'Our Apple accessories, which start at £25 for the cheapest item, are hugely overpriced for what they actually are…' or 'Our strangulation of the music market has undermined record companies and artists and broken the old music business model forever, which means new entrants will struggle still further to make meaningful revenues from a music career.' They would say things like 'This is the previous version, it's a great Mac', 'the newer one has additional features – either way they will both give you what you want…' They would say '£25 is a higher price for a small item, and because it's an Apple accessory, you are guaranteed compatibility, high quality, and value.' They would say 'Apple has transformed music for you the customer, which means buying music has never been easier, and listening to it is more personal, and at a higher quality than ever before.

And the barriers for entry to the music industry have been dismantled forever.'

Okay, with Apple it's easy, isn't it? Are they really the only one? Surely, it's harder for other companies where integrity was never at the heart of what they do? That's the problem. We have worked with many companies, retailers, contact centre organisations, web-based businesses, who have realised that they have large established organisations that, within a short space of time, have a reputation for 'give them a call and they'll give you a discount'. And that reputation has been self-generated. Eventually the realisation sets in: 'We're losing money or we're not making anything like what we could – because of this reputation'.

And that's where we come in. We train a sales model that treats customers in a fair and respectful way, and the salespeople learn to personalise their recommendations and act as ambassadors for their brands – rather than internal detractors.

61% of execs admit their sales managers aren't properly trained in pipeline management techniques.
Harvard Business Review

This can be a painful process. Top salespeople, who have earned fortunes just because the company's reputation is poor, are suddenly out of their depth. They complain or resign. Managers say, 'Our results are dropping for our top salespeople, but our average people and lower performance people are all doing a bit better.' There's a shock. 'We don't like the fact that our top salespeople are not doing as well. They won't use the new structure and we can't make them.' Exactly, because they've been *pissing all over your backs and telling you that it's raining* for years, and their awards and bonuses have contributed to poor staff moral and rewarded the wrong behaviour. Change will be difficult and painful, but if you're serious you will need to do it. If you're not serious, you will be made to do it, or you may very well die a slower but inevitable commercial death.

We once worked for a large brand with multiple call centres. Some were owned by the brand, and some were partner sites owned by global outsourced organisations with contact centres all over the world. The partner sites did very little else but discount, lie and cheat to hit their targets. The only loyalty they had was to keep the brand they were working for by hitting targets. How they did it was entirely up to them. The brand-owned sites loved the new sales model and adapted because they were far more wedded to the company and wanted it to succeed. The partner sites complained because, suddenly, they could no longer employ just anyone. They needed better, more talented people, and in the locations where these sites were, these were tougher to find and afford, which affected their operating model. Yet, the benefits for all the brand's own sites were apparent. A changing business, investing in quality, means more profit, security, and money. If you don't give a damn, then you'll carry on lying to people and making up stuff which devalues what you're selling because you don't care.

We were in a meeting with the client, and were tactfully trying to get across the difficulty we were having helping certain people in these outsourced sites to understand what was required. We were struggling to describe the response we were getting from our training. 'This audience… they're not too…they don't get…well, they're…'. The client filled in the gap for us. 'Pond life?'. Wow. That's what they thought of the people they were partnering with and trusting to sell their products. If they thought they were that bad, why continue engaging and outsourcing your business, to a disloyal (or much less loyal) bonding partner? You might think it beggars' belief? Yet when finance people dominate business strategy decisions and they think it's worth it, as it keeps costs low, aren't they being disloyal to the brands they work for? If the owner, is mostly faceless shareholders and you can move on in a few years' time, then maybe as we have said, disloyal bonding, strategically, is a choice that goes all the way to the top?

Training for loyalty also means you must learn a huge lesson. You are ultimately training many people, so they can leave your employ and get better jobs. You're investing in them in such a way that the connection between training and talent will mean their 'worth' increases, and they may quickly see where better opportunity beckons. This puts some companies off the idea of investing. If they're into control, then it's easier to control people with limited empowerment, enablement and ability. Then they wonder why they can't grow and that's where training comes in. Richard Branson is quoted as saying, "The thing that is worse than training people and having them leave, is not training people and having them stay."

Not everyone wants to be a manager; not everyone wants to climb the ladder. Some people just want to earn more, go home on time and enjoy their lives outside of work. That's their privilege. Enabling them to do that, to be more successful, win you more customers, balance their incentives against your increased profits, this is the objective of some salespeople versus their employers' expectations. That talent that you have grown, and trained must be balanced correctly or they'll go. That brings us back to loyalty. The quick win of money, done in a disloyal fashion, is quickly forgotten when the company starts to struggle, cut back, and uncertainty increases. The salesperson thinks, 'What the hell's gone wrong? I've done my job, hit target, earned commission, won awards, been praised… where did I go wrong?' – and it wasn't the salesperson. It was the company who didn't train them, who operated in a short-term fashion and didn't bother to manage their behaviours.

One of the biggest issues for huge numbers of organisations is managing follow up; going back to customers after they have received a quote. We met with a Senior Director of a major travel brand and explained that her people were not following up efficiently by telephone. 'My Regional Managers have told me, that customers say they don't like being followed up...' That's the tail wagging the dog, isn't it? More likely the Regional Managers have been told that their teams don't like following up because there's low confidence, and actually the Regional Manager doesn't like following up either, so let's construct a disloyal lie that will take away this task that no one likes, even though well managed follow-up is guaranteed to increase business. This is a classic example of a serious training issue being side-lined through a mutinous, disloyal strategy.

Looking at the training your people have received at induction and beyond, would these subjects: Disloyal Bonding, follow-up, selling the brand, personalisation, handling complaints fairly and with integrity and with a speedy resolution approach, enablement, autonomy, profitability and value-selling ever be fully addressed and trained for? If the answer is no, isn't it about time that you re-aligned your learning and development functions and started to invest?

Chapter 10: The Effort of Removal, Recovery and Growth

The Principles of Sales never change, all that changes is the product, the individual, and their ability to translate those principles into profitable results.
Practical Sales Mantra from Reality Training.

Imagine a marketplace that has two major players and hundreds of smaller ones. The first major player, Brand A, has thousands of staff, all using disloyal bonding to sell. On paper and in the City they look really healthy. Thousands of new customers, high revenues. Profits aren't amazing, as the debt level is high, but the acquisition of new customers means nobody is too concerned about that. Brand B is solid, performing well, profits are higher but the acquisition of customers is lower. Debts are lower.

Brand A starts to borrow more and more money. They sell bits of the business off to off-set their losses, which keeps them going for a year or so, and the CEO who signs these sales off, earns a life changing bonus, whilst at the other end of the business small numbers of redundancies are happening, shops and offices are closed and cost savings are being made.

Brand B, ticks along, doing pretty well. They don't make as much noise as Brand A but they don't need to. They also have stronger and better partnerships with smaller players and are largely trusted. Brand A are viewed with increasing levels of suspicion, which affects their business too.

One day, things get serious, and the leaders of Brand A realise they are in real trouble. Why are people buying, but not coming back? Why are they not making any money? Why are they starting to struggle? They engage marketing consultants; they look at their people; they start to train them to act differently. In the meantime, they go back to their shareholders, the City and others, to get short term funding to prop themselves up whilst they change. Brand A may have been operating like this for years. Their staff are going to really struggle to behave differently and do it at the speed needed to save the company and patch up their dying reputation. What are the steps needed to remove Disloyal Bonding?

There are several stages.

1. Leadership needs to recognise that this problem is essential to saving the company. And they must own it, communicate it, and show their support for its removal and their zero tolerance of those who cannot drop it. Any leaders who don't make the change quickly must leave the business, together with any of their lieutenants who have supported them.
2. Marketing messages need to change overnight and move away from price related offers towards value based, integrity focused creativity.
3. All customer facing staff must be trained in the right behaviours, centred around a simple sales model that is customer focused and has no room for disloyalty. This must be supported and coached by their managers and any managers who don't really get it,

and the importance of it, must also leave the business.
4. Approaches for funding must show how the brand is changing for the long-term benefit of all, and that this will cost something, but that the investment will ensure survival.
5. Any customer facing people who cannot communicate in the required way must also leave the business (once this has been fairly proved) and smaller numbers of better-quality people on higher salaries should be employed.

The recovery will take three years. There will be tough times when the temptation will be to be disloyal to the brand again in order to win some revenue, but this short termism means nothing if the brand can't survive. The outcome will be a smaller, leaner, but more profitable Brand A that will be a firm Number Two in their market, because Brand B will be Number One and Brand A will be a solid company that has a future, that can grow again and can also become a respected brand in their market, and that huge change in operation will have been worth it. If a CEO is appointed who wants enthusiasm and growth to be at the heart of the brand, then they've got a great chance. If a CEO is appointed who spends a year getting rid of lifeless and reluctant elements before implementing the changes, then they risk doing too little, too late. If a CEO is appointed to keep the brand going for a few more years to pay bonuses to directors, then the brand is doomed. Additionally, if a 'rescue CEO' is brought in it will be far easier for them to cut back than invest. So, a CEO with no vision is a bad omen. This emphasises why this change must come from the top.

Conversely, there are leading brands who know that they have this problem, that they exist with a poor reputation. They're still successful because their product line is good, but they want to shake off this bad reputation. The implementation of a company-wide structure for engaging with customers is invested in. Within that structure is flexibility to get across personality, but there's no room for disloyalty. Managers are taught how to coach this structure, and to coach the individual in integrity and the right positive and healthy mindset – and anything that goes against the positive principles of the structure stands out immediately. Additionally, this change, for thousands of people, with the inherent high staff turnover, will take three years, and newer people will know nothing else and will get it more quickly than those who have been around a while.

That three-year shift from bad to good reputation will have some tough times. The outcome though, will be a company that is entirely fit for purpose in a way its competitors are probably not. Plus, they will have a structure that is adaptable for the future, and it won't allow Disloyal Bonding back in. They also realise that they will have to pay more money for better, multi-skilled people, who can deal with any type of customer, and this will actually be an investment in the future success they want to ensure. This is the secure business many of us would like to work for.

Chapter 11: The Restaurant – Reboot

I diet between meals.
Michael Winner, Critic and Film Director

What should restaurant service really be like? Waiting staff, Maître d' and the whole team front of house and kitchen and beyond must know about the food and drink they are selling. They should know everything about it. If they don't know all that they should, with some level of enthusiasm, don't let them in front of customers. They should not be thinking about getting through their shift; they should be thinking about making sure the customers love their experience so much that they will come back and tell their friends about this place too. That's the minimum objective every time.

They should also have a level of awareness that is far higher. Is it a celebration? Can we make it a celebration? Can we anticipate what people will be wanting to order? Can we make sure we are attentive to every table, without being over the top? This sounds a bit like a show. Every night you are performing for the diners in a way that will impress them. If you're not up to the show on a particular evening then how can you go on the 'stage', knowing your service will be below average?

The real test for any restaurant is when things go wrong. They will. Plates will be dropped. Waiting times will be too long, popular dishes will run out, customer requests will not be able to be fulfilled. Customers will argue with you, or with each other. How can you deal with these inevitable issues in a way that exceeds the customers' expectations? Or do you deal with them in a way where the customer says nothing, then leaves, never to return? When people vote with their feet, (and Brits are famous for it, we don't complain well on our island!) you can't turn that complaint around. Your ability to deliver when things go wrong is the acid test for amazing service.

We were once in a bar in London and ordered a gin and tonic. The bar tender went over to the gins, lifted the Bombay Sapphire bottle and waved it at us. Were we going to shout 'No! Put that bottle down and pick up the Gordon's, which is 40 pence less per shot?' Of course not. We just nodded sagely as if the bartender had read our minds.

Even in top class restaurants and hotels, you can be disappointed. We had a Christmas party in The Ivy in London, a place that used to be a top restaurant with a great reputation. They knew it was a Christmas party, so this was their chance to sell champagne, wine, cocktails, the full menu and charge a large service fee. Instead, they hurried us through the meal. They wanted us out so they could get another table in. Their way of maximising was to sell each table twice rather than increase the profitability of the table's they had in. For a top restaurant, this is the sort of behaviour you would expect in a lesser chain. It put us off, and we have not returned. We wrote a review on Trip Advisor that was not responded too.

In the USA where hospitality wages are very low, knowing that most leave a tip, the focus is on the extra level of service. But not everywhere. There's a restaurant we've been to in New York where the service was so unbelievably good, it knocked us sideways. All women, all dressed in smart uniforms, their knowledge and common-sense approach to putting you at your ease was amazing. To go to the lengths they went to, to make sure you were having the best of evenings, would take a whole book in itself. Each cocktail could be described using the best possible adjectives. Every dish was known, because every ingredient had been explained. They appeared to take an absolute interest in us, the English couple. One thing they all did was make and own their decisions: they never referred to anyone else and it was impossible to tell who was in charge - they were all superior service level people. Finally, though, when the bill came, there in large letters at the bottom it read 'This is a non-tipping restaurant.' They were that good and they weren't hustling for tips! In the US this may well be unique.

Hospitality is a marketplace where the belief is that they can continue to get away with paying poor wages because for waiting staff and bartenders it's largely unskilled labour. Except, it is actually important to have some skills to deliver the best service. Wouldn't it make total sense to find and train people who can maximise every drink, every food order, every visit rather than simply pay someone to take the money. If a round of drinks costs £20, could we upsell that to £25 every time, with a little skill? Adding 25% on to most orders, would that help some places stay in business? Do pubs and restaurants think so little of their customers that they try and get away with keeping their people's skills at a low level, when the people concerned are more than capable of learning a few simple ways to improve their customers' experience, whilst upselling to them?

The best bartenders have people coming into the bar, because of them. Yes, they like the food and drink, but they like the personality, and the best have customers coming back night after night, spending their money. To close on these real analogies and memories, one of our friends visits a local restaurant that has struggled on for years without changing, and where the staff start moaning about the place, the food, the boss, as soon as you walk in. 'Oh, this place is terrible...' We wouldn't go to listen to this, but our friend goes because he totally loves their cheesecake... but he tells everyone about the Disloyal Bonding – and people think – 'I won't bother going there, then!'

Chapter 12: Tailor Made Service

To buy books, as some do, who make no use of them, only because they were published by an eminent printer, is much as if a man should buy clothes that did not fit him, only because they were made by some famous tailor. **Alexander Pope**

When we meet new clients, one of the 'never to be achieved' objectives that many have is to create multi-skilled customer service salespeople. Right now, they will have siloed departments, so if you are a retention customer considering leaving and you go through to the wrong department, you will be transferred. Many of us will have been transferred to different departments, sometimes between countries or continents, simply because when the call was finally picked up, it was the wrong person in the wrong place.

Imagine going through to a large organisation on the phone, and whoever picks up the call, whatever your reason for calling, they can help you; a well-trained team that are completely knowledgeable and deliver seamless, high-quality service. They just switch the conversation depending on the type of call.

This dream is something we discuss often. But the first task is always to make sure everyone is trained in the best way to engage customers before we even think about multi-skilling. There's the challenge, because some just don't want to be trained, and some can't be trained. You could find people with enough innate talent to be a multi-skilled server, but you'd have to pay them more. If you think about the economics, though, the staff turnover for most organisations is high. One retailer we know had 100% staff turnover of retail staff, excluding managers, every year. Hundreds and hundreds of new members of staff, all year, every year, are new and need training.

Could we really have helped, or is that culture shot to bits? It turns out it is.

This presents a huge challenge which means to multi-skill people on top of other deep rooted cultural problems, namely trusting people and enabling them, is a bridge too far.

We demand better service as consumers. We want to believe that the value proposition for the product or service has been tailored to suit us. That's not too hard to train. If the salesperson can amend their conversational model, then they will be successful, but if they can't, then that won't deliver the change in the right way. The perception is that many, entry level customer service jobs, attract people who would otherwise have got jobs in retail, hospitality, or manual/factory work. There's this old-fashioned, class-led and rather insulting idea that those of us who would have been on the assembly line in factories forty years ago are now working in contact centres. If that is the case, then sadly, our society hasn't moved on much in forty years, and we need to reconsider this assumption. Communication skills are not learnt in school, and unless someone has an innate confidence, or they've got it from their parents, they need to be trained. Most can be trained to take a certain type of enquiry or a certain type of customer. You need to train people differently and far more intensely to be multi-skilled. The solution is this; train them in sales skills. Make sure your staff realise that they're salespeople. Embed those skills. Then add in different customer types and note the differences. Make sure your IT can manage the switching around.

Sometimes the recruitment for customer service people is desperate, especially after something like Brexit and the pandemic which generated thousands of vacancies in the UK alone. When we advertise, we are in danger of attracting just about anyone, and because we must fill seats, we sometimes take them. We then hope that our training will give them the skills, but in truth, as well as you may train someone, if they don't have the fundamentals, a basic level of verbal dexterity and some flexibility, then they will act as low performing automatons, and, in order to maintain their positions, they will be soft touches for the behaviours of disloyal bonding which we have already identified. This means your training and induction must be linked. When they, as a new member of staff are shown the company history, have learned all about the mission, vision and values, such as they are, then the employer must make the connection between those things and the right behaviours, expected of them in their role. If employers are not explicit, then they're cultivating an environment where they are unwittingly bringing in and encouraging the behaviours that will damage our business.

Senior Directors, must, with urgency, experience the customer's perspective for themselves, and then agree to build the customer experience around some semblance of tailoring. Even better would be a senior executive who can experience the services without being known. (As Ellis Watson[*] famously took the Greyhound bus across the US, before beginning his well-documented turnaround of that business.)

An adequate level of service is standard and uninspiring. Surely, we want our people to deliver a tailored experience every time?

The way this is done is by using Value Added Propositions (VAPs). These are different to a Unique Selling Proposition, (USP), a feature or a bullet point.

When Rosser Reeves[*] coined the term USP and wrote about it in his book *Reality in Advertising* in 1961, the focus was all about the uniqueness or creating an idea of a product or service having fundamental unique features that the competition did not offer.

In a way, all products and services were sales pitches. It didn't matter if you didn't know your customer or client's desires; your primary mission was to be skilled in getting across your USP to the buyer so they could be swept up in your product's uniqueness and buy it.

Times have changed. Business buyers and consumers have the internet to research and read about all manner of products and services and the brands that offer them. What they want is to be asked questions and to feel that they have been listened to, and that it is they who are unique.

---

[*] Ellis Watson former CEO Celador, DC Thompson, Celador etc.
[*] Rosser Reeves Advertising Executive and Author.

They have a particular need or desire and when you understand them then, and only then, do they want to hear what you have to say, and you better make it all about them. If you don't, they won't buy, and they'll shop around until they feel someone appreciates that they are a little different to other customers.

The VAP is a value statement that has the customer within it and has this type of construction. 'You told me you want to be able to do X. Therefore, I recommend you get the Y product/service. What that means is you'll be able to achieve Z in half the time and also receive these additional advantages...'

The VAP demands two clear actions from the salesperson. Firstly, we need to ask more questions of our customers, more in-depth, open, unexpected and compelling questions that make people really think and feel. *Not* FAQs - those questions can faq off! We need to be able to naturally ask broad and more in-depth questions. From their answers, we are now able to form value statements that connect the product or service. This works in every channel, face to face, on the phone or over the web. Other VAP examples follow here:

'You told me that you have five people living in your house... So, I recommend/advise/think that you should buy... What this means/what this will give you and your family is...'

The language is entirely flexible – it could be as simple as: 'You said you spend two hours per week checking your books. So, I recommend this accounting software, which does all that for you, saving you 8 hours per month - what could you do with that extra time?'

Or it could be fuller, like:

'You explained that you are now driving 4,000 miles less every year as you've retired, so, I think we should adjust your policy accordingly. So, you will pay less for your policy, but still be fully covered as you enjoy taking trips with your wife, Sue, and your grandchildren.'

Or it could be as complex as:

'You've been very clear about the data issues your organisation is facing, and the crucial consequences of managing this correctly. This management information system allows you to monitor how the data is being utilised and you can maximise time and effectiveness with every division of your organisation, saving you hundreds of man hours every month. What this means is that within three months you will have got back over £20k in productivity, which will feed through to your bottom line and return your investment.'

The internet made it possible for all of us to buy things that we believe are tailored for our specific needs. You can order a car, choose the engine size, transmission, colour, trim, extras, everything you'd want, and then pay for it and have it delivered. You can design a kitchen online, order it, have it delivered and fitted. You can order clothing, suits, dresses, underwear. You can order pieces of IT engraved with your name or spectacle frames and lenses. You can order supplies and software for your business without speaking to anyone and you can specify products and services for your business through online catalogues. With web chat, now we can even negotiate and close people. Soon we will be looking at each other over the web, so the interaction will be face to face – which means the relationship will be stronger and more personal as a result - you would hope. We are all demanding personalisation and as companies, there is a desire that customer's will feel, at the very least, that who they are buying from is delivering something close to that, as a fundamental business goal. If it isn't, then it needs to be.

Disloyal Bonding would state that 'people don't really want that, they don't trust our attempts to bespoke the solution, they just want something cheap...' Back to that perception of what is cheap and what is expensive. As you try and build that tailor made solution, if the customer asks, 'Why are you asking me all these questions?' the answer is simple: 'How can I recommend exactly what you want if I don't understand exactly what you need?'

Let's also remind ourselves of some key facts. You don't have to do business with them. You're not going to sell to everyone or retain everyone - that's impossible. Some customers will cost you more than you get from them. Some customers, you will regret to your very soul. We remember once having a customer who was so foul and unprincipled, we regretted ever meeting them. Even now, twenty years later, we still feel the personal hurt from that relationship, that was only business related.

Understanding your best customer, the one where both the profit and relationship is, is essential. If we didn't try and bespoke their solution, and sold them something generic, and it was wrong, then that would be dreadful and damaging service. Our commitment to helping them get exactly what they would like is likely to save them money or time or deliver greater immediate value, and could keep them as customers for years.

Lastly, it may be that your people have never truly experienced bespoke, personalised service themselves. We were part of a programme for a major automotive company, and another programme running concurrently was an experiential one. They took their people to a top-class Michelin star restaurant, to really study the way they were served, to see the reality of high level, focused attention to the customer. For many, this was a huge learning experience because they realised that they had been short-changing their own customers for years, and this was probably a reason for mediocre performance. Experiencing a tailor-made service is a great way to then work out how to deliver it yourself.

Chapter 13: Integrity at the Heart of Insurance

Don't sell life insurance, sell what life insurance can do.
Ben Feldman

The insurance market is changing. Gone are the days of facing massive, unexplained increases in premiums every year, when you haven't made a claim. Most of us don't like having to buy insurance, we just need to have it, and if we can get it for less, then we will. Now, that dynamic is changing. The emphasis must be firstly on the quality and relevance of the policy, making sure it is exactly right. Then selling the importance of being happy with the renewal and selling the importance of staying with this insurance company (where most of the profits are made in subsequent years, rarely in Year 1 of a policy being sold). The charade of negotiating renewal prices every year will soon be effectively pointless in the UK, which will place integrity, value and price at the heart of this competitive market.

Many of us buy our insurance with the thought 'I'll probably never have a claim.' So, we cut the cover to the bone to save a few pounds, not realising that this could leave us in a difficult situation if we were to have a claim and not be adequately covered. At that point we would have gladly paid the slightly higher premium, but then it's too late. If your insurer had integrity, they would explain that to you, fairly and clearly, so that the choices you made were fully informed. If they simply allow you to cut back your policy without properly questioning you, and explaining the value they are offering, then that shows little or no integrity, even, and this is crucial, if you, the customer, say that is exactly what you want. Sadly, there are "senior" decision makers who are secretly acting as Heads of Disloyal Bonding with well trotted out phrases and even guidelines expressing, "if the customer is happy to renew, just get on with it." It reminds Jeremy of when he was told to 'straight-repeat customers' (advertisers) rather than attempt to upsell them, when the Directory Company he worked for was going through an IPO, (which makes the City your supreme head of disloyal bonding).

In our chapter on the man's tough day of Disloyal Bonding, we showed the meeting in the insurance company, where senior managers realise that disloyal bonding is a lever they can pull to increase conversion rates. It may well be the wrong lever, but they may also be managers purely because they have been using that lever themselves for years, and they know it can help hit a target, tick a box, or make a customer feel that they appear to have been given what they wanted.

There are so many types of insurance these days, critical illness, life, breakdown cover, travel, boiler, buildings, landlords etc. For a long time, as we've previously mentioned, the companies themselves and their multiple brokering partners, accepted that they would make little to no money in Year 1 of a policy. But that Year 2, provided there were no claims, would be mostly profit. Plus, if there was a straight renewal there was zero cost of sale, too. Huge retention teams were developed, many by us, to receive calls from unhappy customers who had just received their inflated quote, ready to negotiate a better deal, not quite as high as the quote they had received, but a little higher than the year before. Now that dynamic will disappear, so the incentive for the customer will change too. For the first time, the agent will have to really get into detail on the policy, the strength of the company providing it and the specific features for the holder. They can't negotiate the price as much, so the detail will be everything. They will be concerned about competitive companies with less integrity flouting the rules to retain customers. This will mean more escalated claims and more accusations of mis-selling, which the insurance industry can ill afford. Only today, while driving, we heard a radio ad asking listeners to get in touch if they had bought a timeshare that they thought had been mis-sold to them - looks like mis-selling continues in many other marketplaces.

The ultimate move will be the insurance brand that brings all family insurances under a single premium, and sells the full cover for everything, for a single price. The combination of insurances would guarantee a saving and save customers and companies time, every year.

The pandemic has also raised the key question about the validity of business insurance and whether it is worth the high premiums for relatively low levels of cover. Business, adversely affected, will be examining their business interruption clauses far more closely from now on and will expect to pay more in the future to get the right level of cover. Who would risk all this disruption again and be poorly insured?

In summary, the insurance market has been forced to change and, over the next decade, that change will also force the behaviours to change. As other markets are forced to abandon previous pricing practices, then the essential addition of value selling to each conversation will benefit customers and eventually make companies more sustainable and less underhand in their dealings with their customer base.

Chapter 14: Loyal and Valuable

The final issue we face with disloyal bonding is that it totally stops us from creating a customer base of loyal and valuable people. Because so few businesses can be bothered to allocate customers to account managers, customers accept new staff every year will be handling their business. Wouldn't it be great if, every year, you spoke to the same person for your renewable subscriptions? They would have made a few notes to remind themselves about you, and when the time comes, they'd use a reminder of last year's conversation. Rather than a brand, you'd have a relationship with a person this time, someone whose professionalism you trust and appreciate. This keeps you as a customer, and they are your annual expert who keeps you informed and happy. Maybe your documents and email should come from them too, completing the connection. Companies would be concerned about customers calling back and querying things and the cost of making sure that that specific person was available to call them back, but if the customer is calling in anyway, it's just a question about how you manage it. Plus, when they do call in, if you're any good you could always try and sell them something else.

When customers complain about value, as they are entitled to, then you employ positive persuasion to remind them of the personalised value they are receiving. You are also strong enough to make it clear that your business is a strong brand, entitled to function as a commercial entity and that, whilst value objections are perfectly reasonable, so is your explanation of these commercial truths, which means they not only understand the value once more but that they can also have confidence in the brand, which for many things has value way beyond the price the customer is paying. What's the point in buying from a brand that is at risk, more risky, less reputable, and then having to start the relationship all over again with a higher priced but stable brand when it fails? The customer doesn't need to agree; they simply need to believe that your intentions are entirely honourable and that you want to maintain this business for the long term. This takes a stronger conversation, an adult conversation. At the end of that sentence, reading it back, we are reminded of the old adage: *integrity in life is everything, if you can fake that you've got it made.* Of course, you shouldn't need to fake it, but for some it may feel like that at first.

If you think about Disloyal Bonding, the customer and the salesperson change positions: from Adult-Child, to Child-Adult, to Teenager-Adult where it normally stays until the end ('Can't you do me a better price?'). Giving in to teenagers is a painful business, so how much better to be Adult to Adult?

This creates loyalty. It creates steady profitability because an annual inflationary rise is the very least you will add, and customers will understand the value of what they are buying and feel better about their buying decisions. They may understand the relevance and safety of buying other things from you.

That loyalty promotes the customer's chances of promoting you positively to friends and family and may also mean they respond favourably to a specific referral strategy because they want others to experience the value you represent.

A man selling baby car seats and buggies in a department store has expectant couples queueing to see him every Saturday. Why? Because he never sells standard seats and buggies. He asks them specific questions about the baby, car, terrain, locality and travel plans. He then sells the seat and buggy for those specific needs, regardless of price, and people pay whatever he asks because his expertise is so valuable - and why would you ever stint when it comes to a newborn baby? He has couples recommending him to others, he is constantly selling, and he uses integrity every time.

There are car salespeople who keep in touch with customers and three years later they call them and say, 'You may still be very happy with your car, but we just had one come in, and I remember something you said to me three years ago about trim colours? You are going to love this car. When can you pop in and have a look?'.

There are travel companies and travel agents who charge a booking fee for their advice and time. It has a value. Why give you lots of ideas and cost saving tips only for you to book your holiday more cheaply elsewhere? Where's the integrity in that? Karma and Reciprocity are the persuaders for these types of sales and they do their best to ensure that you keep customers for the long term.

Companies no longer seem to build relationships with their customers. In the past, our whole economy thrived on the people we knew, who sold us the stuff we needed. We had bank managers who we met with, to advise and help us. We had companies we would go to regularly for the same things, or they would approach us to sell us upgrades.

We may be approached by competitors offering us similar products and services for less, but because we are loyal to our current provider, and trust the relationship we have, and don't trust the ability of this competitor to match that, we accept we are paying a little more to get exactly what we want rather than risking paying less and not getting everything we really need.

The brands that create and sustain customer volume built on value and loyalty will be the robust brands of the next hundred years.

Chapter 15: Ten Takeaways

In this book we've attempted to make you totally conscious of this damaging disease of Disloyal Bonding. In the UK, when he was the King of the BBC Radio 2 Breakfast Show, Sir Terry Wogan was known for his self-deprecatory jokes about himself, the show, the radio station, his colleagues and the BBC. He was really taking the rise out of these things. But of course, he was joking. The whole thing was sarcasm, because it was the most popular show in the country at that time. The humour became what he was known for. 'You don't want to be listening to this rubbish... Ah, yes, what time is our rehearsal tomorrow? Welcome to the coffin dodgers' network!' Sadly, many people a) can't tell jokes and b) shouldn't make sarcastic jokes about their own company because, even with the best of intentions, it sends the wrong message out. Wogan could. In the words of Julian Blake, Jeremy's father, 'He talked brilliant bollocks.' But not everybody can.

Here are our Top 10 Key Takeaways with associated actions:

1. Pay people more money, so they can't afford to be disloyal. Demand loyal behaviours. Or pay more, for better people and expect loyalty and the right level of communication.

2. Make sure ALL staff are trained, so that when dealing with a complainer, a renewal customer or a difficult customer, they never fall back on Disloyal Bonding and make it an important disciplinary issue, which is effectively misconduct. Make sure you recruit people

who can be trained to demonstrate loyalty if you can't get people who understand it instinctively.
3. For contact centres or telesales operations, train integrity into negotiation so your products and services are not devalued whether the customer buys or not.
4. NPS. Reconsider Net Promoter Score as a measure. Why not invest in improving your service levels anyway and set your own standard of what outstanding service is? Just make sure you do it properly and get help to implement it in the healthiest way.
5. Don't assume that everything is expensive. If that's part of your vocabulary then you need to be clear on what you mean: a high price or, actually, something that is not worth the money?
6. Spend time and money working out how to make customers feel good about buying from you. Speaking to happy customers would inform this.
7. Be aware of, and honest about, your internal failings and train your people not to mention them to customers, whilst also trying to sort them out.
8. Disloyal Bonding exists at the highest levels. Coach your entire board to root out and get rid of strategic lies and policies that are damaging. Remove the 'Heads of Disloyal Bonding' swiftly.
9. Empower all your people to spot, report and resolve problems immediately and positively without the

constant reference to hierarchy. Positive staff enablement is key for this strategy.

10. Interrogate your performance data. Are your best teams and managers nothing more than Disloyal Bonding cells? Whose side are they on? Are they slowly screwing up your business without you realising?

Epilogue: How It Really Should Be

At the café after the man has wolfed down his immense plate of fried food…

"Oh yes!' says the Barista, 'everything is recycled here. Very important to us. Plus, ethical coffee!' She points at the brown paper sack the coffee beans are delivered in.

As the man leaves the coffee shop, the delight of what has just happened makes him almost forget the £4.85 price tag for the coffee. If others think its pricey, that's up to them. Ultimately, you're paying to save the World.

As he checks his car in to be fixed, the man explains the problem. 'So, you see, it's a hybrid, but it's just not charging properly, so I am assuming it's something to do with the battery?' The Service Manager doesn't hesitate. 'Well, this is a 2015, so that was quite early for the chargeable battery. The good news is you've saved a fortune so far, buying less petrol. We will let you know the best-case scenario for you to retain the value of your car and ensure its long-term value.'

As the man leaves the dealership, he is pleased that he hasn't been given a load of old flannel and he feels that, whatever the outcome, his car is in the best place to get fixed. Some will say, 'well the guy should have been more honest…' but the truth is, no one knows how bad it is until they check.

As the man's son emerges from the dressing room in a smart, blue, three piece, the father becomes emotional. Firstly, he has never seen his son looking for smart. Secondly, the suit is very high quality, deep blue and looks high priced.

'How much is it?' he enquires, gently. Quick as a flash the assistant comes back with; 'All three pieces, only £199.' This sits in the man's brain for a second. The previous suit was only £129, but this one is a step up in every sense. He ponders the price. What's £70 here or there? For his son to look this good. Isn't it worth every penny? The old hand watches the man's thought process for a bit and then decides to help him out. He sidles over and whispers, conspiratorially, 'Tell you what... I'll include a tie from this rack here, they'll go perfectly with that blue.' The man and his son leave the shop with the suit, a tie, and an unspoken commitment to return for more soon.

In the office, the call to the car insurance company goes a little differently. He explains that his renewal quote is too high and he doesn't want to pay so much. The agent asks him some questions about his annual mileage, the value of his car, the types of journeys he makes, and he adjusts the premium by £20 because of the newly calculated level of risk. The man considers the value and pays it. Before the call is finished, he is asked to complete a survey. So pleased is he, that he has got a little off, and believes his policy is excellent, (especially considering how he drives) that he scores the advisor a 9 out of 10, when usually he only ever gives people 8's.

At the same time his travel insurance renewal is going well, via webchat, too. 'My renewal is £150 per year... I want to pay less.' He is asked about his travel plans for the year, asked about his family of five, and the types of trips they take.

The travel insurance company believe the £150 is actually really good for twelve months piece of mind, for five people taking multiple trips all over Europe and, potentially, the US. Knowing he wants to book a holiday and that the holiday company will charge way more for five people's insurance for two weeks, he justifies the £150 to himself and pays it.

The man then applies himself to some work when the phone goes. It is a broadband company offering to take over his line for less money than he is currently paying. When the agent's system is slow, so that the man's questions can't be answered, the agent explains he is embarrassed and will call the man again when the system is working and they have something even more compelling and more reliable to offer.

As he drives home that evening, he pops into the supermarket to buy some pizzas for the teenagers, as he and his wife are going out for dinner that night. The supermarket now has eight robot cashiers, all manned by one person, a lady in her sixties. As he scans the pizzas, a cheeky chocolate bar and an emergency bottle of red, there is a warning that comes up. The lady walks over. 'Sorry, sorry, yes I am still getting used to these things…' As she punches in her code she says, 'Still… saves you from having to join one of those queues.' She looks at the people waiting to process their weekly 'big shop' at the cashiers' check-out tills.

That evening, he and his wife sit down in a lovely pub for dinner. The waitress walks over. 'Hiya, just to say we're very busy tonight so there's a minimum half hour wait for food… but I can quickly bring you some garlic bread and drinks, now?' Placated for now, the man accepts and orders drinks. When she returns later for the food order, he asks a question 'Where do you get your steaks from?' Quick as a flash she says, 'We use a specialist butcher in Winslow.'

The meal is slightly slow in terms of service. Eventually they order desserts. 'I noticed the apple pie on my way in and I see you have sticky toffee pudding on the menu' he announces, his schoolboy roots betraying themselves. 'Are they home-made?' There is a pause. 'Whilst I'm sorry they're not, the apple crumble is, it's amazing with custard…'

That same evening, whilst they are at dinner, an emergency meeting is being held in the insurance company where the man renewed his car insurance. 'Our conversion rate is dropping.' says the Commercial Director 'For every hundred calls we get, we're only saving thirty-three customers, and that's poor. We need to get is up to 50% at least or we're losing money…' Listening to this, the Sales Manager has a solution. 'That's okay, I'll have a chat with the teams. We need to make the customers believe that they are making the best choice staying with us, so we need to question them closely and tailor the policies more. The average handling time may go up a bit, but it will get us closer to that goal if we deliver a more tailored service than we currently do. We need to make sure our people are on our side, selling the right policies, or we'll lose thousands of policies next year at renewal!'

That night, the man's mind is awash with the conversations of the day he's experienced. As he slips into a restful doze, he reflects that almost everything he has been through today has been really, really, high quality.

As he drifts off into the arms of the angel of sleep, the last thing he thinks is: *good to see businesses with some integrity*.

Final Word

Bob Morrell and Jeremy Blake are the founders and directors of Reality Training Ltd. Their work as sales trainers, management trainers and executive coaches has taken them all over the world. They have trained thousands of salespeople, team leaders, sales leaders and senior directors. They are business speakers who deliver as a double-act and have spoken at association and brand-own conferences nationally and internationally.

They work with a small team, Ann Harris, Lorraine Collins and a larger group of trainers, actors and coaches, to deliver change programmes to national and international organisations who care about their customer engagement.

During the pandemic, Reality Training produced and broadcasted many supporting videos on varied business subjects and offered free executive coaching.

Reality Training also produces and broadcasts three free podcasts: *The Reality of Business*, *The Reality is Sales Training*, and *The Reality of Contact Centres*, available on all the major podcast platforms.

Both are authors of several business books, including *The Brexit Manager*, *The Death of Late Space*, *The Perfect Storm*, *30 Ways to Grow Your Business*, and a number of shorter guides. They write articles for business magazines. They also enjoy writing for their regular readers with their monthly newsletter, *In Reality*. More information can be found at www.realitytraining.com.

Printed in Great Britain
by Amazon